JOB HUNTING MADE EASY

JOB HUNTING MADE EASY

A Step by Step Guide

THIRD EDITION

JOHN BRAMHAM
AND DAVID COX

KOGAN PAGE

First published in 1987
Second edition 1992
Third edition 1995

Kogan Page Limited
120 Pentonville Road
London N1 9JN

British Library Cataloguing in Publication Data

A CIP for this book is available from the British Library.

ISBN 0-7494-1590-8

Typeset by BookEns Ltd, Royston, Herts.
Printed and bound in Great Britain by Clays Ltd, St Ives plc.

Contents

Preface and Acknowledgements

This edition has been revised to reflect changes in legislation and the job market, and it remains a simple guide to job hunting. What cannot be avoided is the work you have to put into getting (and keeping) a job.

Our greatest debt is to Mrs Iris Cox and Mrs Susan Bramham, who had the unenviable task of transposing our random thoughts into the logical and consistent final typed text. In addition, friends and colleagues acted as proofreaders, and we would thank them for their valuable advice and guidance, which contributed greatly to the finished product. They were: Geoff Boyd, Peter Joy, Bob Stapley, Dorothy Fellows, Lynne Newman and Helen Peel.

It is impossible to list the many friends and colleagues who over the years have assisted the development of ideas that have resulted in this book.

Mention should be made of all the candidates who have given us the benefit of seeing them perform when looking for jobs and from whose collective experience most of our advice and guidance have been distilled.

Finally, what is written is our own responsibility – and the views need not necessarily coincide with those of our employer, British Gas plc, Kogan Page, or any of our colleagues mentioned above.

David Cox
London
February 1995

John Bramham
Solihull
February 1995

How to Use This Book

A lot of the advice and guidance in this book will be based on you, the reader, carrying out some activity or completing an exercise. There are several question and answer sessions which are designed to concentrate your thoughts and sharpen your ideas about seeking employment. We have included a number of questions we think you should ask yourself in the special question and answer sessions but we cannot cover every individual's situation. You should use our questions to start yourself thinking along the right lines and then develop your own pertinent questions.

For instance, we ask if you would move house for a job, but it might occur to you that you have friends or relatives in a particular area of the country. If you have, is it worth ringing and asking them what the job prospects are like there or even asking to stay with them for a few days while you look around? If you are not that close, why not ask them to send you the local paper so that you can see what opportunities are available. In this way, from one question *you* can open up a number of possibilities. We will try to guide you as far as possible but we need your active participation if you are to be successful in finding a job.

You can, of course, just sit down and read the book from start to finish and you will gain some benefit. However, if you carry out the suggested tasks as you come across them in the text, we feel you will gain much more from it. Also, some of the activities are concerned with regular tasks which will assist you in finding a job. If you do not intend to work at getting a job on a regular, consistent and sustained basis you should read no further. Finding a job is *your* responsibility and if you are not prepared to spend some time and effort on the task there is little we can do to help.

As you read, have a pen and some paper ready, either to carry out the practical sessions or to make a note of things to do when you have finished a particular section. You will not get the best results if you try to read the book from cover to cover. It will be too much to take in. Each chapter covers a particular stage of job hunting, so have a look at the contents page and get a feel for the areas the book covers. You will notice that we have tried to work through the various stages of job hunting in the order that they happen. Even if you are especially hopeful about the outcome of a particular interview in two days' time you should still be sending off letters to other companies, visiting the Jobcentre and carrying out all the other activities we suggest that you undertake regularly. These activities should continue right up to the time you are offered and accept a job.

Chapter 1

First Principles

The background to job hunting

The past ten years have seen a growth in the number of unemployed people in most western countries. In the United Kingdom over 2 million people are registered as unemployed and seeking work at any one time. There are now more people *in* employment in the United Kingdom but it is also true that the number of people looking for work has increased. In fact, there are now more people looking for work than at any previous time. Jobs are available but the competition to get them has grown and this means that finding employment is increasingly difficult.

Both authors are practising personnel managers with many years' experience of recruiting and appointing people to a wide range of jobs. The advice we offer you has been gained from practical experience. We know what the prospective employer looks for when he or she reads an application form and we know why certain candidates are selected for employment while others are consistently rejected. We are aware of comments from managers and other personnel managers that they have difficulty filling jobs because there are not enough suitable candidates. That is not normally because candidates cannot do the job; it is more often because candidates are not being suitably presented, in other words not selling themselves to their best advantage.

In this book we will be showing you how to:

- Identify where the vacancies are
- Go about finding available jobs
- Complete an application form and a CV (see Chapter 4)
- Present yourself in the best possible light
- Perform at an interview to give yourself the best chance to get the job.

In short, we will show you how to identify the market, package the product (you), and complete the sale.

Increase your chances of getting a job

Why do some people succeed in obtaining employment and others fail?

Successful candidates are:

- Methodical, well prepared and well organised
- Enthusiastic and determined to succeed
- Interested in finding a job and committed to obtaining one
- Knowledgeable about the company and the job
- Prepared to spend *time and effort* to find a job
- Able to learn from their setbacks.

If you look at this list, you will realise that all the factors listed are within your control. Whether or not you fit the description of a successful candidate depends partly on your attitude and outlook. Spend a few minutes considering the attitudes and outlook that you bring to the task of job hunting. Do they need to be changed?

Before you decide to go out looking for a job it would be as well to consider what amount of effort you are willing to expend to achieve your goal. Finding and obtaining a job is a matter of opportunities and chances. Finding employment will entail spending *time, effort and even a little money*.

Before you proceed any further, ask yourself if you are willing to spend enough of all three. What sacrifices are you prepared to make to get a job?

Are you prepared to move around the country?	Yes/No
Are there any areas of the country in which you would not work?	Yes/No
Are you prepared to take a job that you dislike?	Yes/No
Are you prepared to spend time each day looking for a job?	Yes/No
Are you prepared to send letters every day?	Yes/No
Are you prepared to make phone calls each day?	Yes/No
If you are in work but want a change, are you prepared to take a job for less money than you earn now?	Yes/No

There are, of course, a lot of other questions you can ask yourself, for example:

How many rejections will you accept before giving up?

After running through our list you may like to add your own questions and answers to establish just how committed you are to this project of finding a job. We hope you are highly committed because if you are, you will follow our guidelines, and when we suggest you take some action or keep some list, you will stop reading and go and take the suggested action straight away. Good intentions are easily made but you must realise that if three months after reading this book you have started a new job, you will have been fortunate. It can take longer, particularly if you have not worked for some time.

Aim at a realistic time-scale.

Government schemes

At any time there are normally a number of government schemes to assist people in obtaining employment or encourage employers to increase employment opportunities. These schemes are frequently changed and fine tuned, for example, to encourage employers to take on people who have not worked for a period or to take on a school leaver and provide training.

In view of the frequency with which such schemes change, you should check with the Department of Employment and your local job shop to see if there is currently a scheme which could apply to you. If there is a particular scheme from which a prospective employer could benefit, you should ensure you mention the fact in your letter of application. You could adapt the following paragraph:

> 'As I am sure you are aware, the government currently offer a one-year reduction in the employer's National Insurance contribution where an organisation recruits an unemployed person. Having checked the situation I believe you would be eligible for such a reduction if I was appointed to this post.'

The incentive on offer will not persuade the employer to appoint a candidate who is not suitable but it could make the difference in the choice between two suitable candidates. The mention of a relevant scheme in your letter also ensures that the employer is aware of the fact that you have researched the current schemes and that you are aware of the incentives available.

Be methodical

The next disciplines you need to consider are the methods by which you keep track of your efforts to find a job. We will be suggesting throughout this book that you get up and do things, write to people, ring them up, go around and see them etc. We want you to apply some system to this work.

Set yourself some targets. When we suggest that you send speculative letters seeking employment to local firms, why not send a letter at the same time each day? Don't give up or leave the task until you've done your letters and marked up your letter log. (Letter logs are discussed in Chapter 2.) If you do this each day it is likely that your postman will soon be delivering several replies a day to you. Certain firms might not bother to give you the courtesy of a reply, and many of the replies will be polite refusals, but some will be encouraging and one or two may even be requests for you to attend for an interview. We recognise that posting letters through the mail can be expensive – do as many as you can afford and ask the Jobcentre, Social Security office or relatives for help.

Job-hunting centre

The next idea we would like you to consider is the establishment of a job-hunting centre somewhere in your house. Ideally, this should be a separate part of a room with a table on which to write.

Here we would like you to collect all the bits and pieces you will need for your job hunting:

- Writing paper
- Pens
- Newspapers containing job adverts
- Stamps
- Envelopes
- Scissors
- Your career history or CV
- Your speculative letters log
- Your diary.

If you can set a room aside where you can leave your papers, away from the prying fingers of curious children or the well-intentioned tidying of your spouse, so much the better. If not, get all the items together in a box or old briefcase.

The important point is that all the items are together ready for you to start. There is nothing worse than seeing a promising advert for a job and spending 20 minutes finding some decent writing paper, a pen that works and a table that is clear. By the time you are ready to start, your enthusiasm has waned and the time to actually compose the application has mostly been spent getting ready. In those circumstances you are hardly likely to give your best to the application.

Time management

The other area to consider, especially if you are unemployed, is how much time you spend on the search for work. It is easy to get into a routine of late rising, pottering about for an hour or two before doing anything constructive with the day. Days spent in this manner are often quite tiring and also very bad for morale.

We would suggest that at the start of each week you make a plan of things to do during that week. In fact, why not get hold of a desk diary for your home job-hunting centre and allocate your time by planning activities into the diary? After all, this may be similar to the type of time planning you will be required to do in your job. You may even find that this type of activity is much more enjoyable than late rising and pottering about.

You should set yourself targets for each day, and at the end of the day or week review your achievements. Start your day with the most important task, the one most likely to bring success. Always remember to leave some time for unexpected events and chance opportunities. A draft plan is shown overleaf.

Your time management notes will be useful when you reach the interview stage as many prospective employers like to ask people how they spend their time while unemployed. Evidence of constructive and consistent application to your job search will count strongly towards creating a favourable impression.

Regular tasks

- Visit the Jobcentre
- Visit the Careers Centre
- Buy your local paper and get the free papers for possible vacancies
- Send off speculative letters to expanding companies
- Keep your job-hunting diary up to date.

Diary		
Time	*Activity*	*Action points*
9:00–10:00	Check post	Update letter log for any replies received/chase any overdue
10:00–12:00	Send your letters	Update letter log to prospective employers
12:00–1:30	Lunch	
*1:30–3:30	Visit post office Visit Careers Centre Visit Jobcentre	Need more stamps Ask about further studies Ask about employment training vacancies
3:30–4:30	Visit central library	Check local paper for relevant news and vacancies Prepare list of firms to visit tomorrow
4:30–6:30	Tea	Feet up, watch local news on TV
7:00–9:30	Visit relatives and friends	Social visits, but ask if they know of any forthcoming vacancies at their firms

Notes
*Must ring city council for information in preparation for interview next week

Enjoy yourself
Your job search can also be enjoyable. You should enter into the idea of rewards for yourself during this time. For instance, don't sit down and try to plough through as many speculative letters as you can because you will not feel that you've achieved anything at the end of the time. Do a maximum number, which should all be written out with envelopes and the details entered on your log. Then reward yourself with a break by going out to the post office or letter-box to post them! Never take your break before you have

finished a task as it will still be there when you come back and, of course, we all find reasons not to go back to half-finished jobs.

We would suggest that you now follow this sustained piece of reading by going to set up your job-hunting centre, perhaps combining that task with a visit to the shops to buy a desk diary, pens, papers, stamps and so on. Return to this book either when you feel fresh or whenever you have that activity next booked into your job-hunting diary.

What type of work do you want?

When looking for a new job try to choose areas of work which are on the increase. If you decide to apply for jobs in a growth area, there are many more chances of obtaining employment than if you pick a declining industry. Even with today's high levels of unemployment there are shortages of suitable people in certain skill areas where firms cannot recruit enough employees to carry out the work that needs doing. Aim to get a job in one of those areas if at all possible. Common growth areas are new technology, computers, electrical consumer goods like video recorders, record players etc and also service industries such as tourism, restaurants and hotels. We are all aware of those industries which are in decline and while there are still opportunities with them the chances are limited, and as we try to stress, you don't want to limit your chances.

Try these questions:

General

What type of work would you find interesting?

Do you want to work with people?
If so, consider voluntary work or, alternatively, a job which involves meeting people.

Do you want to work with your hands?
If so, consider learning a craft; people will always pay for craft skills.

Are you interested in obtaining further qualifications?

Can you afford to delay earning money while you get them?

More education or qualifications?
If so, consider further education courses.

How long are you prepared to spend studying?

Can you study on your own or do you need help and perhaps supervision?

Depending on the answer, consider either evening classes or a correspondence course.

Are you just leaving school and think you need some work experience to enhance your career prospects?

If so, consider enrolling on a Youth Training scheme. Go for a large, well-respected, local firm if you have the chance, as you are more likely to get better training and the experience will count more with other employers.

Be your own boss?
Do you want a lot of responsibility and freedom to be your own boss?

If so, consider self-employment ... but doing what?

The work environment
In what sort of organisation would you like to work; for example, one which makes a profit, one that helps people, an office or service etc, or one that does a little of each?

Depending on the answer, select the organisation appropriate to your needs. When you get a job with a suitable firm you will find you settle in more quickly if the firm's outlook is compatible with your own.

What type of surroundings are you looking for in your workplace? Warm and comfortable or outdoors in the open air?

What type of people do you want as workmates? Young people, people with similar interests, lots of different people?

Do you want set hours, flexible working hours, freedom at weekends and in the evenings?

Do you want security, the prestige of working for a large organisation, or a smaller firm where you know everyone?

Do you want an active job, an artistic one, one with a co-ordinating role, or one where you produce something?

What would you really like to do? Can you realistically expect to achieve it?

What would you not like to do?

Now analyse each of your answers and decide what they say about you and then analyse each and every job to see if it will suit you.

Sell yourself

When you are looking for a job you are trying to sell the prospective employer a package and that package is you. As Robert Louis Stevenson said: 'Everyone lives by trying to sell something.'

Today most people live by selling their talents, abilities and special skills. Like any sales person you must make sure the product that you are marketing appeals to the prospective purchaser. Throughout the book we will be stressing that you must *sell yourself*.

Remember, an employer may have to spend between £6000 and £20,000 a year on a new employee; in addition there are other employment costs which can mean that the total cost of employing someone can be up to three times the annual salary. With that type of expenditure the employer wants the best and is determined to see that he or she gets value for money. Your task is to convince him or her that you are worth the money and that he or she is getting a bargain even to be allowed to employ you. Nobody else can convince the employer of that except you.

You must do this by selling yourself

If you can discover what the prospective employer is looking for then you can start to model your product to fulfil his or her needs. All the clues are available. It just needs a bit of thought and application to discover them.

Identify your strengths and weaknesses

The next exercise we would like you to undertake is to ascertain your own strengths and weaknesses, so that you can then concentrate on what to improve and what to tell a prospective employer. Many of us have a tendency to belittle our abilities and our skills. A lot of this comes from the British trait of modesty. This is all very well when you have a job, but when you are applying for employment you have to be the one candidate out of a pile of 20 or even 200 applicants who really impresses the prospective employer.

When we advertise a vacancy the normal result these days is to be overwhelmed by the number of applications. When there are 40 applications to be looked through, given that the people concerned are normally busy, each application will only be studied for at most 30 seconds. The quickest way to do that is to look for reasons to *exclude* people. Therefore, what happens is a quick reading of all the applications rejecting any that do not meet certain basic standards. It might be something like not living in the catchment area, no experience, not being suitably qualified etc.

If you have not identified and sold your strengths but have instead concentrated on listing your weaknesses you will be one of the first to be thrown on to the reject pile. You will not even have the opportunity to go for an interview to convince the interviewer that you are the right person. The most difficult aspect of getting a job is getting the interview. You must impress the employer on paper long before the interview. List all your strengths. Stress them and overcome your weaknesses.

You need to sell yourself

For instance, if you know you live quite a distance from the place of employment, tell the employer how you intend to deal with the travel problem. Look at your application critically and ask yourself what the problem areas are. Then explain to the prospective employer how you intend to overcome the problem. If you cannot think of a way to overcome the problem then you should not be applying.

Turn your weaknesses into strengths

Most of the things that you consider as weaknesses, if looked at in a different light, can actually be classed as strengths. Remember, we all have our own strengths and weaknesses. Let's have a look at a few examples.

Some people see themselves as indecisive. To others they appear careful; they avoid making rash decisions. This strength is often valued in a job where the employer is looking for a careful employee.

Another example of turning your weaknesses into strengths is to consider the question of age. Many people feel that at a certain age you are past the stage where you are suitable for some jobs.

However, rather than putting that on an application, why not make your age into a strength?

> 'I appreciate that I am aged 45 and may be older than the ideal candidate you are looking for; however, I feel my greater age and experience of life would allow me to bring a mature and settled outlook into your organisation which may complement the other younger people that you employ.'

You are actually suggesting to the employer that he or she needs somebody with a bit of age behind him or her to offset the many young people there may be in the organisation.

Alternatively, many school leavers feel poor examination results may stop them obtaining a worthwhile job. Remember, interviewers also had to sit exams and may not have done particularly well. Also remember that most interviewers know that whatever you learn in the fourth and fifth forms about maths, geography, history, Latin and biology will have very little relevance in your daily work in an office, factory or shop environment. However, basic skills are vital. If you can add, subtract, divide, multiply and calculate percentages, that is enough. Most offices today will provide enough calculators to assist with even these basic skills and if the organisation you apply to does not provide them, buy your own. Instead of apologising for your poor results, why not try to make a virtue of them?

However, a word of caution to any school leaver. It is well worth remembering that if you have good exam results and a pocketful of GCSEs, then you do not have to excuse your results. Only get yourself in the position of having to make excuses for your results as a last resort!

We hope that with these examples we have convinced you that many of the things that you consider weaknesses in your application can in fact be classed as strengths from a different point of view. It really is a matter of looking at your circumstances in the best possible light. Why not spend 15 minutes now looking at yourself with a view to converting any weaknesses into strengths? Relatives or friends could help you, as they will be inclined to see you in the best light, whereas we all tend to be over-critical about our own abilities and weaknesses.

Recognise your strengths and shout about them

One area of strength which many people ignore is their personal interests outside the field of employment. On most application forms you will be required to supply details of your personal interests. Is anything you do in your spare time of relevance to the job? Again, the school leaver with poor exam results and a poor academic record may well be undertaking some kind of work at a youth club. What the interviewers will be interested to know is, does that person just go along to the youth club or does he or she actively take a part in running and contributing to the place? Alternatively, does he or she have a spare-time job like a paper round or undertake any work organising committees?

You should always stress any activity that indicates a level of responsibility or concern for other people and an interest in what goes on around you. If you bring those qualities to a job they could well make you a good prospective employee.

Many people who run one or more mail order catalogues in their spare time fail to declare that on their application forms. Surely, if you can run one of these complicated businesses, keep track of the payments, what goods you have had in, what goods you have given out, who has paid what and who owes what, you can undertake most office-based jobs! As long as your paperwork for the catalogue is up to date then you are operating as a small business. Anything an office job could throw at you should be no problem.

Of course, some of your hobbies may be turned into a profitable area of work. For instance, if you are interested in animals, keep a few pets, have you ever thought of going into a job where you could use that skill, ie veterinary assistant at your local People's Dispensary for Sick Animals or even (if you get A level maths) a veterinary surgeon?

We all have strengths; we really need to concentrate on bringing these out when we are applying for jobs. You need to attract the interest of the prospective employer and convince him or her that you are the best person for the job. If you do not, nobody else will. The other candidates are too busy telling the employer how good they are.

One of the key attributes people look for in candidates is a willing, enthusiastic person. You must sell those qualities to a prospective employer. Almost anybody who does not know how to do a job can be trained to do it. Many of the qualifications people ask for from candidates are not strictly necessary. Our view is that an enthusiastic, well-motivated person can achieve anything in a job. Lazy people may be well qualified and well trained but if they are not interested in our job, we are not interested in them.

You must impress the employer with your enthusiasm and willingness to undertake any work offered.

Checklist for success

Increase your chances of getting a job:

- Be methodical
- Be prepared to spend time, effort and money to find a job
- Set up a job-hunting centre
- Get a diary and use it
- Use your time carefully
- Set yourself daily targets and routines and stick to them
- Analyse what type of job you want
- Sell yourself
- Stress your strengths
- Look at your weaknesses and turn them into strengths
- Reward yourself when you have finished a task or routine.

And, above all, make a job out of getting a job.

Chapter 2

Finding Jobs

Where are the vacancies?

Chapter 1 stressed that finding a vacancy and obtaining the job is greatly assisted if you think positively. The first way to increase your chances is to strive actively to find out where the vacancies are. There are many methods of doing this. Many vacancies will occur and be filled without most people taking the trouble to find out about them. If you find a vacancy which you think is interesting you should try to ensure that you are the first person and preferably the only person to know about it!

The busy manager will quite happily appoint the one and only applicant for a job if he or she is satisfied with that person. In fact, if the manager knows of somebody suitable, he or she may not even bother to interview but be quite happy to bring him or her into the organisation as quickly as possible. When somebody leaves or an organisation requires a new employee it invariably wants someone immediately. As personnel managers responsible for recruitment, we are all too aware that every department wants its vacancies filled tomorrow (if not yesterday). If a vacancy is advertised in the local press, followed by interviews and medical examinations, it can take up to three months to recruit someone in a large and complex organisation. But if someone's name is already on file who is interested in the type of work available there is a great temptation to appoint that person without the rigmarole of the full recruitment process. A more immediate response to filling vacancies is very common in smaller companies, also shops, hotels, bars and fast-food centres, where the luxury of a long delay is not acceptable. For this reason the smaller organisation may be more receptive to a speculative personal approach.

Be first to find vacancies

Many firms realise that if they advertise they will get a wider selection of applicants and may even end up making a better appointment, but quite often, because of pressure of work in most departments, they will accept someone who is available and ready to start straight away provided the person looks good enough to do the job. Remember, many firms do not normally advertise vacancies they can fill by word of mouth. Your task is to find out about the vacancies before other people do and make sure you are available.

In all your contacts with organisations you should always provide a telephone number where you can be reached. If the firm is looking for temporary assistance, and you are on the telephone, it can make the difference to whether you are contacted to attend for interview or not. If there is insufficient time to write to applicants and six suitable candidates are on the telephone, those six will be contacted. Of the six contacted one or two will be unable to attend and the remaining lucky or diligent four will be asked to come for an interview. You then have a one in four chance of obtaining a job.

Remember also that large and small firms differ in this respect. A small firm may be free of trade union agreements and extensive bureaucracy and be more willing to appoint direct. Because of this the speculative application directed at a smaller firm could have more chance of success than a similar application to a large organisation.

Families, friends and word of mouth

These are some of the best ways of finding out about vacancies. We all have a lot of personal contacts, the majority of whom work for a living. You should actively ensure that all your personal contacts, all your relatives and all your friends, are aware that you are looking for work and the type of work in which you are interested. You should make a point of notifying them of your interest, either in a friendly conversation or by ringing them up if you have not seen them for a while, and asking them to let you know of any potential vacancies.

You should never see a friend or relative who says: 'I wish I'd known you were looking for a job; there was a vacancy at our place last week, but it is filled now.'

Not only do your relatives and friends know when vacancies arise, they also know when they are short-staffed at work, when they are doing a lot of overtime and when people are ill or on maternity leave. You should capitalise on that type of information.

If you know that a factory or office has more work than it can handle, for whatever reason, you should be phoning, writing or personally visiting that place to register that if a vacancy exists you are the person for the job and can start straight away.

In addition, your friends, relatives and contacts will be aware of people they work with who are due to retire. Make sure that you have applied to that organisation specifying that you would like to be considered for any suitable vacancies that come up in the near future and try to make sure that when that vacancy does arise you are considered for it.

Alternatively, if you already have a job and you are interested in changing, make sure that any customers of your current firm or any contacts in other firms working in the same field know of your interest and are keeping you posted on potential vacancies. Should you be lucky enough to be selected for an interview by one of these firms where you have a personal contact, make sure you ask that person to tell you all about the organisation before you attend for interview. This is a point to which we shall return in the section on interview preparation.

Remember that this is how many jobs get filled, so work on your family and friends.

Libraries, directories and *Yellow Pages*

In any area of the country there are libraries which can offer information on local firms, or careers in firms. You should, if you are unemployed, spend a morning in the library doing some research on which firms are in the area. If you are looking for work in the hotel field, copy out the lists from Yellow Pages and write, ring or visit the hotels listed. One of them will have a vacancy which might just suit you.

Many areas are now covered by local directories such as those issued by the Thomson Organisation, and these are useful lists of business classifications and addresses. Take a page at a time and work through, contacting each and every firm that may offer you employment. As we stressed earlier, if you send one letter of application you are unlikely to obtain employment. If you send a hundred you are much more likely to find a firm with a vacancy! You should aim to send something between one and a hundred. Arrange to issue as many letters or make as many telephone calls per week as you possibly can. There are jobs available; you just have to find them.

Application letters

You should regularly write a number of speculative letters to organisations within your area. It is best to set yourself a target of so many letters per week and carefully maintain a log showing to whom you have sent them. An example of a suitable log is shown on page 28. This will allow you to keep track of how many applications you have sent, who has responded and who has offered you a further opportunity to find a job. For instance, if a firm says it has no suitable vacancies but will keep your details on file for six months, then in five months' time you should write back and ask if there are any suitable vacancies yet.

In deciding your target companies you have to make sure they require the sort of skills you have to offer. You can also increase your chances if you know that a particular company is in the market for new employees. Companies who have recently been recruiting or who are successful or expanding are always good prospects. For this reason ask the Jobcentre which companies are in this position. Other sources of such information are included in the list of useful contacts on page 109.

Apart from assisting in your methodical search for employment the log of speculative letters is extremely useful when you attend for interview. Most employers like to interview and appoint people who are keen and willing to work. Therefore a common question will be: 'What efforts have you made to find employment? If you can show a high level of systematic application of effort to getting a job, then that is a strong point in your favour. When asked how many jobs you have applied for, show the interviewer your speculative letters log. Tell him (or her) that on a regular basis every day you send off seven letters to local firms. The interviewer will be impressed by your hard work, your methodical approach and the amount of time, effort and money devoted to finding a job.

A draft speculative letter is included in Chapter 4 which covers applying for a job (see page 53).

Telephone calls

While it is not always appropriate to telephone to ask if any vacancies are available it can occasionally pay dividends. Quite often you will be put through to a busy office who will tell you that you should write expressing an interest. Ask to whom you should address your letter and have a pencil and paper ready. A

Letter Log Page 1			
Date sent	Organisation	Reply received	Comments
1/2/95	Smiths Import & Export	15/2/95	Nothing suitable try again in 6 mths, diary noted
1/2/95	Local council	18/2/95	They will keep my details on file
1/2/95	Jones the builders	12/2/95	Application form to complete, returned to them 12/2/95, good chance of an interview
1/2/95	Sharps Wholesale		Phone tomorrow if no letter received
1/2/95	Water Board	9/2/95	Interview 20/2/95 Research still to do
1/2/95	Electricity Board	12/2/95	Nothing suitable try again in 6 mths, diary noted
1/2/95	Local press	18/2/95	Nothing suitable try again in 6 mths, diary noted
2/2/95	Local supermarket	19/2/95	Details of trainee management scheme, it would mean moving. Application sent back 19/2/95
2/2/95	Heavy metal merchants		Phone tomorrow if no letter received
2/2/95	Police Force	10/2/95	Interview date 1/4/95. Research to do, would local police help me with my enquiries? Must ring and ask them

speculative letter addressed correctly to the manager by name will have more impact than a letter addressed to 'Dear Sir'. Also, when you write, refer to the telephone call to ensure that they are aware that this is your second contact with them and thank them for being so helpful on the telephone.

Alternatively, out of ten calls that you make each week you may be lucky to be put through to a person who has just been notified of a vacancy. You may then be lucky enough to be considered for a vacancy which will not be advertised, or sent to the Jobcentre or Careers Centre. You are then one jump ahead of all the other people seeking employment in your area.

Visits

Spending a day going round various factories, offices or likely places of employment asking if they have any vacancies can be productive and relieves the boredom. You may be stopped by the gateman/commissionaire, or by a clerk from the personnel department or the manager's office. You may get nine refusals from ten visits. However, again you may just be lucky enough to knock on the door of a particular firm when they have a short-term vacancy which has just arisen and they need somebody urgently. Even if this is unsuccessful and people tell you to write in, refer to your visit in your letter.

This approach can be hard work and is likely to be more productive if you target the right companies before setting off. Organisations to concentrate on are the ones who have recently announced expansion plans or ones where you know a vacancy has recently arisen.

Tell people when you go for an interview that once a week you visit organisations, looking for employment. Again, the interview panel or the prospective employer will be impressed by your enthusiasm. Also, if your are unemployed and you really want to work, can you think of a better way to spend day than going around looking for a job? It may be frustrating, it may be disappointing and you will probably get a lot of refusals, but you could end up with a job.

Careers Service

The Careers Service provides a job-hunting service for people leaving full-time education. It tends to concentrate on school leavers aged 15 and 16, each year either trying to find them a job or a place on a Youth Training scheme (YT). Given the overwhelming number of school leavers each year and the few vacancies notified to the Careers Service, it does a very good job with limited resources. However, most vacancies are not notified to the Careers Service and this should only be used as a supplement to all the other methods of identifying opportunities that we have listed in this chapter.

Jobcentres

This is a free service provided by the government to help organisations publicise their vacancies to those people interested in a new job. The Jobcentres try to provide a service to all people looking for employment, those who have jobs and those who have not. However, they also help those people looking for work to whom the government is concerned to offer special help. Such groups as the long-term unemployed, the young unemployed, people wishing to move from an area of high unemployment to an area of low unemployment, all have been the subject of special schemes at one time or another. The schemes on offer can be complicated and poorly advertised but you should spend some time looking at the leaflets and talking to the staff, who are very helpful, to find out if there is a special scheme for which you qualify. If the government has a scheme to help people in your situation you should ensure that you benefit from it.

Jobcentres operate by offering employers a service of displaying vacancies at no cost to the employer. A card is displayed on a notice board in the Jobcentre giving details of the vacancy and both unemployed and employed people can browse through the cards. If they wish to apply for a particular vacancy they obtain further details from a receptionist. Jobcentres are very useful; they may have a number of vacancies notified by certain employers, but for one reason or another some employers will not use the service at all.

You should find out when your Jobcentre receives new vacancies, ie which is their most popular day, and arrange to visit at least on that day. However, for the best results there is no reason why you should not visit the Jobcentre each day, particularly if you are not currently employed.

One disadvantage of Jobcentres is that by the time you have seen a vacancy advertised on the notice board perhaps up to a hundred other people all looking for employment may have seen it too. The other disadvantage is that a vacancy in one area may only be advertised in one Jobcentre whereas people in other areas may be quite willing to travel to the job but they will never find out about that particular advertisement.

Recruitment advertising

Many firms advertise in local and national newspapers, although this is often either for a highly paid job or alternatively for a job which is difficult to fill. Certainly, if a clerical vacancy carries a large advertisement in local papers the firm may well be inundated with applications. For a clerical vacancy it would be more useful either to use word of mouth or alternatively go to the Jobcentres. Therefore, if you see an advertisement in the paper it will normally either be for some scarce skills or abilities, or there will be a large number of applicants. By all means apply, but the competition will be tough.

Most local papers have a certain night when job vacancies are advertised and you should ensure that you get a copy that night. However, some firms advertise on other less popular nights, possibly to reduce the numbers of people responding. If possible, you should arrange to get the local paper every evening or as early in the day as possible. If there is a suitable vacancy advertised then apply as soon as you can. This is urgent because the firm may have decided to accept the first 30 or so suitable applications. Make sure your application is one of the first 30 that they receive.

Employment agencies

Employment agencies are normally commercial organisations which make a living from matching an employer's needs to the details held on a number of candidates. The vast majority make their money by charging the employer a fixed fee, in the range of 10–25 per cent of starting salary, for finding the best candidate for a vacancy. Some employers use employment agencies for nearly all vacancies above a certain level, whereas other employers will not use an agency but do their own recruiting. If you wish to register with an agency make sure that there is no built-in charge to the candidate but merely to the prospective employer. Based on the fact that some employers only notify vacancies to their employment agencies it may well be a good idea to register with a number of agencies.

Employment agencies also supply temporary staff, when requested, to other businesses and can often be a very useful method of obtaining short periods of employment with different firms. There are two advantages for you in this system. The first is that in a short time you can gain entry to a number of organisations, all of which represent an opportunity for employment on a permanent basis. The second advantage is that during a relatively short period you will gain experience of a number of working situations which could strengthen your application for permanent jobs. This second advantage could be of particular benefit to someone returning to work after a break in employment.

Job-hunting diary

We have now discussed various ways of finding where the vacancies are, all of which require some time and effort from you. We suggest you now use the summary at the end of this chapter and book each activity into your job-hunting diary which we talked about in Chapter 1. Remember, do not overestimate the amount of work you can do in a given time. Set yourself realistic targets and reward yourself when you have completed certain tasks. Be flexible. If you plan to spend a day making personal visits to places you think may have vacancies, make sure that the next day you have booked something that can be done at home. In the event of bad weather on the first day you can swap the activities and avoid wasting time.

Checklist for success

- Many jobs are filled by word of mouth
- Use your personal contacts – they can be vital
- Always leave a telephone number where you can be contacted
- Libraries, *Yellow Pages* and trade directories can supply details of suitable firms
- Send speculative letters each day
- Telephone calls can produce offers of interviews
- Personal visits impress employers and can be enjoyable, but target the best companies first

- Use your Careers Centre and Jobcentre
- Get the newspapers and apply early
- Use your time wisely and use your diary
- The more enquiries you make the more likely you are to find a job
- Discipline will stop your enthusiasm tailing off
- Remember to keep your log, be methodical and *enjoy yourself!*

Chapter 3

Returning to Work

This chapter is directed at those people who for one reason or another have a break from formal employment. Most commonly this will be a mother who has decided not to continue working after childbirth. However, men could also find themselves in situations in which they have been unable to stay in full-time employment. The break could be for reasons other than a need to stay at home to rear children. Charity, political work, caring for aged relatives or perhaps a long-term break caused by redundancy can lead to difficulties in readjusting to the discipline of full-time working. We say 'discipline' in order to make clear that we recognise how much hard work is involved for people who, according to statistics, are not part of the 'working population'.

What special problems exist for the person who wishes to return to work after a break of some years? These revolve around out-of-date skills, lack of current working practice, poor or nonexistent qualifications, and the residual problems that may result through personal circumstances. This chapter will suggest ways of dealing with these difficulties and conclude with a personal development and time management programme in order to impress upon a prospective employer the seriousness with which you are approaching this matter.

Are you out of date?

It is important to recognise that change may seem to occur slowly and usually imperceptibly, but change nevertheless takes place. People who return to work after, say, 10 to 15 years appreciate this. Office, shop and factory procedures and attitudes will have changed significantly. Laws and regulations (relating to food handling or safety requirements, for example) have undergone significant change, and much of what you learned some years ago is now out of date. If you do not realise the extent of the changes, your old knowledge can even be dangerous to prospective employers.

It is important to acknowledge to a prospective employer where you will need to learn new techniques and practices. It is even better if you can demonstrate that you have kept up to date. If you want to work in an office, or in retailing, buy the trade magazines for a few months and see what is going on. Every occupation has trade journals and the articles give you knowledge of current trends and problems.

Technology and change

In the area of technology anyone who was not working two or three years ago will see a dramatic impact. New technology is making many skills redundant, particularly those requiring quick fingers such as filing-card handling or assembly work. One dramatic example is the supermarket check-out where dexterity, speed and accuracy were once crucial and sought-after skills. The bar codes now on most retail products are leading to automatic checking of prices by machine. Make sure you know of the technology – take the trouble at interviews to ask if they offer systems training. Show you know what is going on.

What sort of job?

Before you go after a job, think hard about the sort of work you want to do. The hardest decision is the level you are going to aim for. Some soul-searching is necessary here and it is rather like the decisions that have to be made by 16- and 17-year-old school leavers.

In summary, are you willing to take a relatively low level 'pin-money' job or do you aspire to supervision or management posts? This is important because many employers will offer mature entrants training and development opportunities, such as taking exams set by the vocational institutes (say, personnel, marketing or legal officers and so on).

Some jobs will be such as to enable you to decide on the question of advancement after a period of time, but others may have no route for more responsibility. It is unlikely that any advancement is possible without training and development which will involve personal commitment. This brings us to another key area.

How is your education?

One problem many people face who have not worked for some years is that attitudes to training and education have changed. While technology takes the dexterity and drudgery out of many jobs, there has at the same time been an increasing demand by employers for people with an ability to solve complex problems. These can occur equally to a part-qualified teacher's assistant in a primary school, an estate agent's clerk, in retailing, or in dealing with customer enquiries in the builders' merchants.

The increasing demand for thinking skills in otherwise junior jobs has led to a recognition of the importance of education. You will have to take some decisions about your education, particularly if you left school or your last job with few if any qualifications.

Get qualified

Fortunately, it is possible to widen your educational scope. There are many part-time courses available from those covering specific skills to the high-level general education available through the Open University. Remember that even a period of studying, say, office procedures and practices leading to no formal qualification, is a valuable pointer to a prospective employer. It shows your commitment to yourself and your job.

How important is your work to be?

Finally, since you are starting again, think hard about what you really want to do. This goes back to Chapter 1 when we discussed personal needs. In short, the decision revolves around how important you want work to be in your life. The 'pin-money' job is useful and will make few demands on you outside the time at work. The other way you can use casual employment is as a gentle method of re-entering the job market.

The relative lack of responsibility means that when you leave work you leave the job. However, if you aspire to more demanding positions, the extra rewards you seek have to be earned. The problems you might encounter in a senior position can include:

- You cannot leave the job behind
- Problems come home with you
- You might be called upon at odd and inconvenient hours
- Supervision lands you with other people's problems

- Training might be during evenings and weekends.

Having said that, the benefits of management responsibility, such as deciding how a job is done, sorting out problems and helping people, and the additional remuneration, are considered by many people ample and significant reward.

Coping with residual problems

You will have to sort out for your own benefit (and for your prospective employer's) how you will adapt your lifestyle to regular work.

If you have children, they may no longer need constant minding, but arrangements to look after them when they are off school or ill will have to be made. Without being discriminatory, an employer will want to know that you can handle any difficulties without landing the firm with frequent and unreasonable levels of absence. This is particularly important in the smaller company. A shop with five staff cannot afford the regular absence of one of them. For this reason it is important that your family is behind you in the move you are making and fully supports it. Make sure that you have worked through the implications for your family. They should know what effect your job will have on them. Incidentally, at any interview the prospective employer will want to see evidence that you want the job and not just the money.

Apart from your employer, it is important that this question is resolved for your own benefit. Money can be a pressing need to return to work, but a high price can be paid in emotional and domestic upset if you do not adapt your lifestyle to regular work. You should not expect to do all you did before and work as well. Either the housework suffers or it is shared among all the family. Make this clear at the start!

Are you up to work?

Having agreed that work in the home is often ignored when people ask 'Do you work?' it is worth recognising that there are differences. These difference show up in the disciplines that work imposes. It is one thing to be able to work diligently, as home or voluntary work implies, but the strict disciplines of office, factory or shop work give you an added burden.

At home, for example, it is possible to take a few hours off, or defer a task (the ironing!) until a more suitable moment. At work this kind of flexibility is much less frequently available. For an employer the person who can 'get on with the job' without constant moans or questions is the employee that is required.

You have to decide whether the type of work you want is the kind that fits your natural inclination. Then you have to show the employer that you can do it. As a piece of training for yourself it is perhaps worth setting disciplines on timekeeping and management of jobs and keeping to them at home. An employer would be most interested in seeing such personal development and time management programmes of the types referred to in Chapters 1 and 2. You can then explain that your purpose was to train yourself for regular work and to be able to demonstrate to yourself, your family and an interviewer that you understood what was needed and that you could do it.

Applying for jobs: special rules for non-workers

This section is additional to the general principles in Chapter 1 where we discussed applying for jobs in general, and to the greater detail in Chapter 4. The aim here is to highlight the problems of the so-called 'non-worker'. Basically, this revolves around the fact that a lack of current involvement in paid employment and perhaps not having worked for many years leads to a thin and out-of-date application form.

A common statement on application forms from married women, for example, is as follows:

> 1978–1989 Office Supervisor Department of Energy. Left to have a family.

The form is then left blank after 1989 showing that the person has had no worthwhile experience since that date and is now applying for employment in a clerical sphere some years later. Incidentally, the example of a married woman is given to represent a problem that can apply to men and women.

We often hear this type of statement from people being interviewed on the television, 'I'm *only* a housewife.' However, being a housewife and mother is in itself a difficult and tiring task which probably exceeds the commitment required from any office job. Let us have a look at that application again.

A revised CV

1978–1989 Office Supervisor Department of Energy. Left to have a family.

1989 to present. I have been a housewife for the last six years concerned with running a household for my husband and two children, now aged six and five. During that time I was called upon on a daily basis to be a manager of a unit of four people, a teacher of two enquiring youngsters, to provide first aid and comfort when needed and also to hold disciplinary interviews when appropriate. Following these six years' experience when the working hours often exceeded 14 hours a day, I know that I am more than qualified for any office work that you can offer.

1995 PTA Member and School Governor.

Add to this a full CV as shown in Chapter 4, together with the evidence of your personal development plan on education, updating your knowledge and time management. You are now getting somewhere.

Plan your comeback

Let us put all this together into one summarised strategy for your return to paid working. At this stage we will not consider the tactical problems of actually getting the job – these are set out in detail in Chapters 5 and 6. We are concerned here with the general principles prior to sending off your application.

- *What do you want to do?*
  What type of job do you want?
  Can you do it?
  Do the jobs exist and are you likely to get one?
  How important is your work to you?

- *How are your qualifications?*
  Do you need a high level of education?
  Is it likely to help you get a job?
  How much time will you put aside?
  Apply to your Adult Education Centre.
  Try Open University (OU) non-degree courses.
  How about an OU degree?
  Do you want to (can you) study at home or college?

- *What about your training?*
  Have you any skills in your target area?
  Can you get additional skills in advance?
  Can you get skills through voluntary work?
  Take part-time work to ease yourself in and show what you can do.

This may sound hard work, but work is. At least the odds are on your side - the major growth in jobs these days is in the field of retail/service/office/part-time work and this is likely to be just what you are looking for.

Checklist for success

- Find out if you are out of date
- Recognise your limitations
- Technology may have left you behind - check
- Think through the sort of job you want
- Eduction and special skills are important - so get qualified
- How much is work to be the centre of your life? The answer affects the jobs you can aim at
- Will family considerations predominate?
- Work out possible snags and solve them
- Is your family ready for the change?
- Stress at interviews that you have spent the last years working
- If you need skills or qualifications start years in advance
- So plan your comeback!

Chapter 4

Applying for a Job

Getting ready

Before looking at this subject in detail, it may be advisable to deal with a piece of jargon you may come across in your job hunting which we mentioned briefly earlier. 'Curriculum vitae' (CV) is a Latin phrase which literally means 'schedule of your life', and is really a personal history. The term in recruitment circles refers therefore to a summary of what you have done and what you can do. An example of a CV is provided on page 55. It is occasionally referred to as a resumé – a term popular with American companies.

When applying for a job either by a speculative letter, a CV or an application form, remember that you are putting together an advertisement to sell a product, and that product is you. First impressions count and this will be the first information the prospective employer will see. Think of the person who will receive the letter; he or she is a real person after all. Try to imagine yourself receiving the application. What would you expect? What standards would you set? This person has never met you before and you must sell yourself by supplying a full application with all the relevant details to impress a complete stranger.

If all of these warnings seem to sap your confidence, do not worry. Some time and effort must be applied to all stages of job hunting and if you follow our advice then your application, be it a speculative letter, a CV or an application form, should be of a high standard. To emphasise the point, it should take you up to two hours to draft an application, get it checked by someone, redraft it to incorporate their comments and complete the final version.

If the procedures for completing applications seem somewhat daunting, you can start right now with the initial preparation. We would suggest that you prepare a personal profile in your job-hunting centre. On a piece of paper, write down:

- Your personal details
- Your qualifications
- Your previous training
- Your job history to date
- Your previous experience
- Your personal interests.

If you are not sure about specific dates of previous employment or exactly what qualifications you obtained, go and find the original documents now, as when you come to complete a speculative letter, a CV or an application form, this initial preparation will stand you in good stead.

Getting good references

One other aspect of preparation is to decide who you will nominate to provide references to support your application. The majority of organisations ask for the names and addresses of two people who are willing to supply a reference. Normally, the first name should be that of your current or last employer, with the other being someone who has known you personally for some time. If you have never had a previous job or it was some time ago you can always supply the name of two people who will supply personal references. You should, of course, select these people with care. They should be people of some professional standing whom you can rely on to respond to a request for a reference, and in a suitable manner. A reference supplied on a piece of scrap paper in poor handwriting will do little to enhance your application.

You should obtain permission before supplying someone's name as a potential source for a reference and keep them aware of which jobs you have applied for. This small courtesy costs little and you may require their services at a future date. Also, they will be able to tell you which firms have asked for a reference and this may be an additional source of information to monitor the progress of applications.

A good reference is someone who can vouch for you, particularly in the area of work for which you are being considered. The person should be someone with status like a doctor, lawyer, business person or head of a voluntary organisation. If you are leaving school, the head teacher, class or year teacher is the normal person to supply a reference. It may be an unwelcome point, but teachers can make or break you at the application stage. Go and see them and ask for their support, despite anything that may have happened in the past.

Preparing your personal profile

Having collected all the information regarding the 'This is your life' file you may think you are in a position to apply for the job. However, please do not sit down and try to complete a speculative letter, a CV or an application form straight away. What you need to do is to ensure that you supply all the relevant information in a logical, orderly fashion without becoming too long winded, which could lose the interest of the reader. If you are working on the rough draft of your application as we recommend, you can alter the layout until you are happy it is the best presentation of the information that you can possibly manage.

Once you have finished with your rough draft you should arrange for a relative or close friend to read through the letter, CV or application form. Alternatively, you may wish to get a neighbour who does not know you very well to read through it and give you his or her impressions. We strongly advise you to do this as what you are trying to say in the application form may be perfectly obvious to you but not to somebody else reading the application. When we have been training people on how to apply for jobs and have read through their applications in their presence, the conversation has gone something like:

> 'This applicant has had no previous experience of this type of work.'
>
> The applicant, who is in the room, has normally said:
>
> 'Ah, I worked in a shop when I left school, but I did not put that on the form as I did not think it was important.'

The point we would make from this experience is that when an employer is reading your application form you will not be sitting in the same room. You will not be able to answer any queries that he or she may have regarding your application. If information is not on the piece of paper the employer will not be aware of it, and will assume that if you have not stated something it is because you have not got that particular experience or qualification.

Another common error on applications is to list the numbers of exams taken without stating pass or fail or the grades obtained. The assumption then springs into the mind of the suspicious interviewer that the grades must have been poor or, alternatively, that the applicant failed the exams. The only reason that candidates do not supply information would appear to be because it puts them in a bad light. Therefore, if any information is missing we assume the worst! Make sure your application provides all relevant details and that when a stranger finishes reading your letter, CV or application form, all questions about you can be answered.

Remember, these documents are a full statement of all your qualifications, experience and capabilities and should be the best advertisement for the product, you, that you can possibly devise. You are asking a potential employer to spend any amount up to £20,000 a year, in wages and other employment costs, and in fairness the employer needs to know exactly what he or she is likely to get for the money. Look again at your forms. Would you spend that much money on the person the form describes? If the answer is no, then improve the description.

If you do decide to get your speculative letter, CV or application form checked, and you should, please accept any points that your adviser makes in the spirit in which they are given. The great temptation is to be offended if someone criticises our work, but surely it is better to accept the criticism than for an unpolished document to be sent to an organisation. The organisation will not criticise your document and tell you what is wrong with it; they will just reject you if it is unsatisfactory. *Take advice and act on it.*

The application form

There is a temptation to fill in just your name and address on the application form and then to write, 'See attached CV'. *Do not do that.* It annoys the person shortlisting. He or she wants a complete set of application forms giving all the same information in the same place, which then makes comparisons easier. Interviewers and people who shortlist are only human - do not make their life difficult.

When you receive an application form you should get the form photocopied and try to complete the photocopied form first. Most local libraries and many shops now provide a photocopying service and copies can be obtained for a fairly low cost. If you cannot obtain a copy then start in the first instance with a fresh piece of paper and try to draft out the application form.

You should read the instructions on the form very carefully. Many applicants fail to realise that we ask for the form to be completed in black ink so that when the form is photocopied and sent to a manager for consideration it can be read; other shades and colours of ink do not photocopy well. After having tried to read an application form which is very faint because the applicant has not followed our instructions we would suggest that that candidate is unlikely to obtain an interview.

Similarly, most application forms start by asking for the surname in the left-hand corner and forenames on the right-hand side. Candidates who put their forenames in the wrong box do not present a very good image. Read through the application form very carefully. Does it request completion in block capitals only? Does it request that you complete the form in black ink? Does it require you to list your previous employment starting with the most recent position etc? If you handwrite an application, please ensure that other people can read it. Even neat and attractive handwriting can be illegible to the unfamiliar. Ask someone to check your handwriting for legibility (and spelling)! Remember these are important documents.

You should, of course, structure your application form to reply to the particular advertisement. In this way you can emphasise any of your characteristics that appear to be specially relevant to the job. Therefore, we would recommend that you do a separate individual application for each different job you apply for. Having read the advert you should know what the prospective employer is looking for and you should structure your form accordingly. It may well be worth doing some research on the firm before you apply so that you can stress any previous experience relative to their operation, or express some interest in the particular work with which they are involved. Remember to stress your strengths and minimise or play down any weaknesses. Make sure you follow any special instructions on the form, like quoting a reference number, and make sure that you get right the job title of the post for which you are applying. Remember also, your application form will be subject to an often cursory sorting process by a busy personnel manager or personnel director looking quickly at all prospective applications. Make sure your application form is placed on the shortlist pile. Make sure you answer all the questions and don't waffle. If you really want the job, you must complete the form.

The other important point is to ensure that you complete the form as soon as you receive it and return it well before the closing date. If an organisation is swamped with applications within the first five days of the appearance of an advertisement, they will often consider the first ones received and shortlist candidates for interview from those early applications. Make sure yours is one of the first back in case this happens.

Quite often there will be a space or an opportunity on the application form to add additional information. *Use it.* Make sure you list anything that you think the application form has omitted to ask, or that might be of interest to the prospective employer, any reasons you might have for being interested in that particular vacancy, any experience, specialist knowledge, training courses or personal qualities particularly relevant to the vacancy, for instance. You should also provide the reasons for leaving your last job or seeking a change, your availability for interview, your earliest starting date, current salary and any future salary requirements you may have.

Once you have completed your draft form and revised it until you are happy that it can be understood by a perfect stranger, you should then complete the original form or prepare your final CV or speculative letter. One thing we would emphasise is that the form must be kept clean, tidy and neat. If you have followed our advice and have a job-hunting centre set up, you will have a suitable place in which to work. However, whatever your own circumstances, you should make sure that the form arrives at the organisation looking clean, tidy and uncrumpled. There should be no coffee or food stains on it. These points may seem obvious and we should have thought they were, but many of the forms that arrive in our department seem to have been used as a rest for a hot coffee cup. Make sure you remember to sign and date your form if required. The next step is to post it to the correct person at the correct address, cross your fingers and wait.

Be neat

You should ensure that any form that you send off is legible and neat. If your handwriting is really bad then you may wish to consider typing your application, CV or speculative letter but you should be warned that many organisations like to see a hand-written form. We would suggest that you handwrite the form, particularly if you are applying for a clerical job. However, if you are applying for a more senior job which would normally have secretarial support then typing the form is acceptable. Alternatively, if you are applying for a typing job then you should type the form as an example of the work that you could produce if appointed.

If you make a mistake on your speculative letter or CV you should start again, so that the finished product is mistake-free. Obviously, the application form should, if at all possible, have no alterations or crossings out and no spelling mistakes. However, we are all human and sometimes once a mistake has been made there is no option but to cross it out neatly and correct it. Again, when the form is completed, please ask a friend or close relative to check it carefully with you for spelling, overall presentation and general layout.

There are other points to remember.

- Use black ink, it photocopies well
- Complete all the sections on the form, do not leave any gaps
- Do not misspell words used in the advertisement
- Get the company and manager's name right
- Do not add any sheets; fit it on the form and if necessary offer to expand the information at the interview.

Normally, advertisements appearing in the press or at Jobcentres will ask candidates to obtain an application form and reply by a given date, although some advertisements may include a request that candidates send for details of the vacancy or to apply by phoning the firm.

If you are asked to write in to obtain details of the job and/or an application form there is no need for an elaborate letter, just a single sentence or two should suffice. There is an example on page 48 (letter X).

Preparing good speculative application letters

As mentioned above, you should begin by drafting the key points of your letter which you want to use before you decide on the final format which you will send off. There is some advantage in trying for an individual approach rather than being just the same as all the other letters that firms receive each and every day. One interesting letter which we received is shown on page 49 (letter Y).

Obviously, you can use this letter as a guide but other ideas will spring to mind and some kind of individual approach quite often works. Remember that the letter you write must be relevant to the company. However, as we have tried to stress, people who carry out recruitment are individuals. Some of them may well think that your fresh approach is of interest and shows some individuality, while others could think that it is cheeky and impertinent and may

Letter X

7 Chelford Close
Parkside Estate
Liverpool L23 2WE
Tel (0191) 263 4539

12 May 19XX

Senior Personnel Officer
Smiths Import & Export
120 Reading Road
Liverpool L1 2LA

Dear Sir

Word Processing Reference XYZ

With reference to your advertisement for a word processor in the 'Chronicle' on Friday 7 May, I should be obliged if you would send me further details and, if appropriate, an application form.

Thank you for your assistance.

Yours faithfully

J T Davies (Mr)

well treat your letter in a similar manner. But gimmicks work and can separate you from the crowd. If you do decide to go for some kind of unorthodox approach, why not check it with some friends and neighbours first, before you commit yourself?

Write short and clear letters

Your letter must be clear, to the point, and should specify the type of work for which you would wish to be considered. It is extremely difficult to deal with a letter which just asks for any type of work. Although you are leaving your options open, the employer receiving the letter does not quite know where your true interests lie. While it is recognised that some people may accept any job, it is difficult to shortlist someone for, say, a van driver's vacancy if all the company has received is a general speculative letter. If your application is too general you may end up not being considered for a vacancy for which you would have been particularly suitable. Therefore, we strongly suggest that you start your letter by stating which type of work you would consider.

Letter Y

7 Chelford Close
Parkside Estate
Liverpool L23 2WE
Tel (0191) 263 4539

12 May 19XX

Senior Personnel Officer
Smiths Import & Export
120 Reading Road
Liverpool L1 2LA

Dear Sir

Do you believe in miracles?

Well I do and I hope you will be good enough to help to make my miracle come true. Leaving school these days, and with the high numbers of unemployed people, it is often only by a miracle that an individual can find a job. However, I am very keen to obtain clerical employment and if you can help me I would be most grateful.

I left Liverpool comprehensive school in June of this year with nine GCSEs in the following subjects:

Maths	grade B
Geography	grade C
English Literature	grade C
English Language	grade C
Biology	grade C
Physics	grade C
French	grade C
Chemistry	grade D
History	grade D

I have always wanted to work in an office and I am particularly keen to get into the import and export business. I feel sure this is an exciting area of work involving as it does assessing demand both in this country and abroad. You will notice I have a GCSE grade C in French and I feel sure my knowledge of this language would be of some use in working for your organisation.

If you are in a position to start the first stage of my miracle I would be most willing to attend for an interview at any time to suit you.

Yours faithfully

J T Davies (Mr)

If that statement is in the opening paragraph the person reading it will be able to make a decision very quickly as to whether they have any suitable jobs for you. If they do not have any suitable vacancies at the moment they may not read any further but may arrange to file your letter in case any vacancies arise in the future.

If the firm writes to you and notifies you that your letter will be held on file remember to make a note on your speculative letter log and in your job-hunting diary to remind yourself to contact them again after a suitable interval to check if any vacancies have arisen. However, if the firm does have a vacancy they really need to know whether you are qualified for the vacancy or not and you should then list your principal qualifications. Do not limit yourself to academic qualifications; list such things as a clean driving licence, number of years' experience in this type of work etc. Make sure that if they do have a vacancy in your chosen field, you immediately provide them with the right information which proves you are the person for the job. Remember, the person trying to read 30 or 40 speculative letters each day will be trying to deal with your letter quickly and may well be trying to push it on to the reject pile. Your main task is to stop that happening.

The other important aspect, of course, is the layout of your letter. If we look at letter A and letter B (on pages 51 and 52), how many GCSEs does each candidate have?

We think you will agree that candidate B, who actually states how many GCSEs he has and lists them in the vertical manner, is much easier to remember than candidate A, who has listed them horizontally. Remember, the person reading your letter may not go through and count up your exam results, so tell him or her how many you have. Also, candidate B looks as though he has more qualifications than A because the way he has set them out takes up more space. The recruiter may well count up candidate A's qualifications but subconsciously candidate B will be remembered as the better candidate. The letter is like an advertisement, and advertising is all about people remembering your product rather than your competitor's.

Note how at the bottom of the speculative letter we have printed the name and title underneath the space for the signature. This is because some people's signatures are extremely difficult to read or, alternatively, people do not tell us in the letter if they are male or female, which causes problems when we need to write to them.

Letter A

7 Chelford Close
Parkside Estate
Liverpool L23 2WE
Tel (0191) 000 0000

12 May 19XX

Senior Personnel Officer
Smiths Import & Export
120 Reading Road
Liverpool L1 2LA

Dear Sir

I am writing to ask if your organisation has any clerical vacancies. I left Liverpool comprehensive school in June of this year with GCSEs in Maths, Geography, English Literature, English Language, Biology, Physics, French, Chemistry and History.

I have always wanted to work in an office and I am particularly keen to get into the import and export business as I feel sure this is an exciting area of work involving as it does assessing demand both in this country and abroad. You will notice I have a GCSE in French and I feel sure my knowledge of this language would be of some use in working for your organisation.

I am 17 years old and in good health.

I look forward to hearing from you in the near future and would like you to know I am free to attend for an interview at any time.

Yours faithfully

A Candidate (Mr)

Writing a good letter

The speculative letter on page 53 covers most of the points we have made and includes most of the information we would like to see in such a letter.

Mr Davies has started by supplying his telephone number in case the firm want to contact him quickly, has rung up to find out to whom he should address the letter and has started the letter well by showing he is aware of what the firm does and the recent news regarding their possible expansion. Mr Brown, the personnel officer, will quickly realise that this is not a standard letter but one specifically written to Smiths. The impression is confirmed as Mr Davies uses the firm's name later in the letter and shows he really wants to work for this firm.

Letter B

8 Chelford Mews
Parkside Estate
Liverpool L23 4QT
Tel (0191) 000 0000

12 May 19XX

Senior Personnel Officer
Smiths Import & Export
120 Reading Road
Liverpool L1 2LA

Dear Sir

I am writing to ask if your organisation has any clerical vacancies. I left Liverpool comprehensive school in June of this year with nine GCSEs in the following subjects:

Maths	grade B
Geography	grade C
English Literature	grade C
English Language	grade C
Biology	grade C
Physics	grade C
French	grade C
Chemistry	grade D
History	grade D

I have always wanted to work in an office and I am particularly keen to get into the import and export business as I feel sure this is an exciting area of work involving as it does assessing demand both in this country and abroad. You will notice I have a GCSE grade C in French and I feel sure my knowledge of this language would be of some use in working for your organisation.

I am 17 years old and in good health.

I look forward to hearing from you in the near future and would like you to know I am free to attend for an interview at any time.

Yours faithfully

B Candidate (Mr)

7 Chelford Close
Parkside Estate
Liverpool L23 2WE
Tel (0191) 263 4539

12 May 19XX

Mr D Brown
Personnel Officer
Smiths Import & Export
120 Reading Road
Liverpool L1 2LA

Dear Mr Brown

I noticed in the 'Evening Echo' on Tuesday 10th May that Smiths Import & Export have just been awarded the Queen's Award to Industry and that the firm is expecting an increase in business activity as a result. In view of that news I am writing to ask if you have any clerical vacancies.

I left Liverpool comprehensive school in June of this year with nine GCSEs in the following subjects:

Maths	grade B
Geography	grade C
English Literature	grade C
English Language	grade C
Biology	grade C
Physics	grade C
French	grade C
Chemistry	grade D
History	grade D

I am 17 years old and although I have no previous experience of this type of work I have always wanted to work in an office. I am particularly keen to get into the import and export business as I feel sure this is an exciting area of work involving as it does assessing demand both in this country and abroad. You will notice I have a GCSE grade C in French and I feel sure my knowledge of this language would be of some use in working for your organisation.

In my spare time I am actively involved with the scouting movement and I believe that the responsibility and maturity that the scouting organisation instils in young people would stand me in good stead in working for Smiths Import & Export.

I look forward to hearing from you in the near future and would like you to know I am free to attend for an interview at any time. Also I am free to start work at any time that would suit your firm.

Yours sincerely

J T Davies (Mr)

As we advised, the letter quickly specifies in which type of vacancy the applicant is interested and then moves smoothly on to the applicant's strongest point, his exam qualifications, which are laid out to give Mr Brown the exact details quickly.

The candidate then acknowledges his greatest weakness, his lack of experience, but deals with it by showing how keen he is to get this particular job and by connecting his skill in French with the job he would be expected to do. His next paragraph supports the idea that he has other qualities to offer by linking a spare-time interest with some of the things an employer would be seeking from a school leaver, ie responsibility and maturity.

Finally, not wishing to lose Mr Brown's interest, the candidate winds up by telling him when he is available for interview and when he can start work.

On the basis of that letter we would expect Smiths Import & Export to interview Mr Davies if they have a clerical vacancy or even to see him if they do not with a view to considering him for anything that might come up in the near future.

One last point on speculative letters: please take the trouble to invest in some good quality writing paper. After spending all this time and effort on preparing a good speculative letter do not ruin all the effort with cheap paper or a page torn from a notebook. You would be surprised how many people do use the strangest notepaper to apply for jobs.

Curriculum vitae or CV

We mentioned this term at the beginning of the chapter. Your CV should be a picture of your life to date, concentrating and detailing the points of interest to a prospective employer. If you have a lot of previous work experience, your CV will be very detailed. Even a school leaver can offer a lot on a CV and it is often a useful exercise to sit down and list your strengths and weaknesses prior to completing the CV.

There are professional firms in the market at the moment who will give advice on how to create a good CV and if you are aiming for a senior job it might be a worthwhile investment to ask one of these firms to look at your CV. We would suggest that our previous chapters on how to find a job should be the first starting point. If you are looking for a career in marketing it might be worth getting a professional, glossy-looking CV produced. The choice must rest with you as to whether you feel the expenditure is

Suggested CV

Name	Mr John Trevor Davies
Address	7 Chelford Close Parkside Estate Liverpool L23 2WE
Telephone number	(0191) 263 4539
Date of birth	2/3/1978
School attended	
1/6/1989 to 23/4/94	Liverpool Comprehensive
1/6/1983 to 25/5/89	Cricklewood Junior
Examination results	
9 GCSEs	
Maths	grade B
Geography	grade C
English Literature	grade C
English Language	grade C
Biology	grade C
Physics	grade C
French	grade C
Chemistry	grade D
History	grade D

Personal details
In my spare time I am actively involved with the scouting movement and I believe the responsibility and maturity that the scouting organisation instils in young people would stand me in good stead in any career.

justified. However, when an employer asks applicants to supply a CV, yours must be suitable.

You will need a short covering letter to go with your CV outlining the type of work in which you are interested.

Remember, if there is a reference number given, always quote it, as otherwise your application may be misfiled, particularly if the company has a large number of vacancies at the same time.

One final point to make on all these methods of applying for jobs: keep a copy of what you send to a particular organisation. The information you supply will form the basis of your approach and you will need to refresh your memory regarding exactly what you said before attending the interview.

Telephoning the company

Many advertisements will ask you to telephone for further information about a job and there are a few basic rules to follow in this activity. The main points are:

- Get organised
- Make sure you have a quiet, peaceful room to yourself from which to telephone
- If you are using a public phone make sure you have enough change available or, even better, a phone card that can be purchased in post offices and shops
- Have a piece of paper and a pen ready
- Write down the name of the company you are ringing, the person to whom you want to speak and what you are going to say about your application for the job; it's easy to get mixed up
- You should write down a list of your strengths which are relevant to this job, one or two questions you would like to ask, and have thought through the answers to any questions they might ask you
- Have your CV ready to hand
- If you are invited for interview, write down the date, time, place and the name of the person you are to see
- If necessary, ask for directions to the place of interview
- When finished, repeat back the information you have been given to summarise it.

If you have done your preparation properly the call should go something like this:

> 'Hello, is that W Brown's, the furniture shop? I would like to speak to Mr Jones regarding the vacancy of shop assistant. I saw the advertisement in the *Echo* last night.'
>
> 'Mr Jones speaking. I gather you are interested in our vacancy, what do you think it involves?'
>
> 'Well, probably making sure everything is set out properly and that the furniture is polished, clean and well displayed and correctly priced before the shop opens. Then dealing with customers after they have had time to look around, answering any enquiries they might have and, if they decide to buy, taking the money, doing the paperwork and, if it's a large item, arranging delivery to their homes.'
>
> 'Yes, that's about it, although we would give you some

training before you got involved with the money and paperwork aspect. Have you done any similar work in the past?'

'Yes. I was working in the local supermarket between 1970 and 1978, until I left to have a family, so I am well experienced in dealing with the general public, the awkward ones as well as the pleasant ones.'

'Well, that sounds like good experience, because we do get the odd awkward customer as well and our sales staff have to be able to cope without losing their tempers.'

'Don't worry, we worked with the idea that the customer is always right so I am sure I could cope. Could I just ask if you would need me to work on Sundays for stockchecking or to set the shop up for sales?'

'Yes, we would, although no more than six times a year and we pay double time. Would that be a problem?'

'No, we used to work far more Sundays in my last job, and it was a nice break to have my husband cook the Sunday lunch.'

'Good. Well you sound just what we are looking for. Can you call round for an interview and I can then make a final decision? After that we can talk about hours of work, pay and when you can start. Can you be here for 2.30, 12th of August?'

'Yes, certainly; that's 2.30, 12th of August. I have made a note of that and look forward to seeing you then, Mr Jones. Thank you, goodbye.'

It sounds as though that lady has almost got the job. Would you have done as well as she did? You might have done if you had followed our advice on reading the advertisement and preparing for the call. It is surprising how often people fail to handle such calls well, although if you are not used to the telephone you may well be nervous. The fact that you are after a job and talking to a stranger adds to that feeling of nervousness. You can give yourself an edge and avoid the worst mistakes, like running out of change or having no pen and paper, if you follow the advice above.

Points on job advertisements

Advertisements, particularly in the press, cost an organisation money. What may look like a number of standard phrases and expressions are often only used after a great deal of thought and consideration. The key point is that there are certain expressions used which give a candidate an indication of what the organisation wants. For instance:

> Applicants must have GCSE maths and English or equivalent.

As opposed to:

> Candidates should have GCSE maths and English or equivalent.

In the first advertisement it is unlikely that a candidate without maths and English GCSE or equivalent would be interviewed. However, the second is not quite so clear-cut and leaves the door open for candidates who have not got these qualifications. If applying for the second job, provide a covering letter which should say something like:

> I appreciate that your advertisement stated that candidates should preferably have maths and English GCSE or equivalent but I feel my practical experience of the type of work involved more than compensates for the lack of these formal qualifications.

Therefore, after reading a job advertisement we would suggest that you sit down and make a list of essential and desirable items it mentioned, ie:

- Must have CSE maths and English — essential
- Preference will be given to candidates with GCSEs — desirable
- Candidates must have six months' previous experience — essential
- Applicants should be good communicators etc — desirable

Alongside each essential or desirable requirement, assess your own abilities. Jot down your relevant qualifications, any experience you may have, how it is relevant, and use this information as a basis for completing your application form.

Do not be put off from applying just because you don't exactly fit the job specification or because you think you stand little chance of getting the job because a lot of people will apply. Complete the application form and send it in – that is the only way you will find out whether or not you will get the job. The one certainty in job hunting is that if you do not apply you will definitely not get the job.

Do you mention salary?

This must be handled with care. You may currently, or in your last job, have earned considerably more or less than the employer is thinking of. You may be discounted as a candidate on either ground.

Our advice is that you need not mention salary at all in your application. This is particularly the case if the prospective employer has not mentioned it.

If a salary is mentioned, you should make it clear that you are attracted by it and something in that area would suit you. Obviously, if you are determined to have a higher salary (particularly when you are currently in a secure job) you must make that clear. Inevitably, you will choke off some interviews and you need to think whether that is sensible. This will depend on your circumstances. The salary question is referred to again when it comes to negotiating actual salary in Chapter 6.

Checklist for success

- Get good references and have them standing by
- School leavers should get teachers on their side to give good but not untruthful references
- Be neat and tidy
- Include all your relevant strengths and stress them
- Supply a telephone number
- Keep your letters short and specify what type of work you want
- Try a unique approach
- Prepare your personal profile and your CV - 'This is *your* life'
- Spend time on rough drafts of your applications and ask friends and relatives for their opinion
- When using the telephone make sure you follow our guidelines
- Read the advertisement carefully and all the instructions on how to apply
- If you do not fit the advertisement, explain why you can still do the job
- Return applications quickly
- Keep your job-hunting records up to date.

Chapter 5

Preparing for the Interview

The first reaction on receiving a letter which says that an organisation is interested in interviewing you is probably one of pleasure, and quite rightly so. You have been selected for an interview on the strength of your application and no doubt there are other candidates who have been rejected. So you have cleared one of the hurdles to finding a job and you are still under consideration for that particular vacancy.

Once the initial pleasure has subsided, however, you need to concentrate on your next objective, which is to attend the interview and be offered the job. Remember, all the other candidates will also have that objective in mind. Getting the interview was one task; getting the job requires more concentrated effort and application.

Don't worry; we can supply some advice and guidance.

The interview invitation

The first point that we would make is always attend the interview, even if you are not very confident about your chances of obtaining that post. The experience will be useful and you can always learn something new about your interview technique. Perhaps more importantly, you may impress the interviewer with your abilities and it is not unknown for a candidate interviewed for one job to be offered a different post. Remember that and go in and do your best.

Some firms, particularly if they are in a hurry to appoint someone, may have telephoned you with details of the interview. If they have, you need to give the impression on the telephone of someone who is well organised and capable. Therefore, when the telephone rings make sure that the television is turned off, the dog is out of the room and not barking down the phone, and you have a piece of paper and a pen ready. On many occasions colleagues have telephoned applicants to invite them for an interview and remarked: 'That sounded like a mad-house - kids screaming, people shouting. When I spoke the candidate didn't seem to know what I was talking about. He kept grunting and mumbling and didn't write down the details. I doubt if he will turn up and if he does he will be late or at the wrong place or on the wrong day!'

Establish a good telephone manner

Of course, your telephone manner is not like that but some candidates will arrive at the interview having already made a poor initial impression on the interviewer, and he or she will spend half the interview trying to correct that impression. Your telephone technique should be more like this:

'256 3434.'

'Good morning, my name is John Smith, personnel officer with United Fruit Importers. Could I please speak to Mr Jones?'

'This is Mr Jones speaking. What can I do for you?'

'It's about your application for a job with us, Mr Jones. We would like you to attend for an interview on the 26th of March at 10.50. Can you attend?'

'Yes, I can attend. I'll just make a note of the time and date. That's 10.50 next Wednesday morning the 26th. Is that at your offices in Great Portland Street?'

'Yes, that's it. Just report to reception at the main offices.'

'Can you tell me who will interview me, please?'

'Certainly. It will be Mr Fulthorpe, sales manager, and myself from personnel.'

'Thank you. I've made a note of that and I'll look forward to meeting you, Mr Smith, at 10.50 next Wednesday. Thank you for calling.'

We think you'll agree that this conversation is likely to give an impression of a keen candidate who is organised, even helping the personnel officer, who almost forgot to mention where the interviews were being held. Note how the candidate repeated the time and date and had a pencil and paper ready to make notes.

If the invitation to attend the interview is in writing make sure you read the letter carefully, gleaning all the possible information from it. Let's have a good look at the letter or notification asking you to attend. Does the letter tell you who is interviewing? If so, memorise names and job titles; it gives a more friendly atmosphere if you can refer to people by their names. Also, if you know their job titles you will be able to understand their questions in the context of the organisation. For instance, in the example above, we would expect Mr Fulthorpe to be asking questions regarding candidates' attitudes and sales ability, whereas Mr Smith could be dealing with candidates' motivation and drive, why they want to change jobs, why they want to work for that company etc.

You may wish to write a short letter to the company acknowledging receipt of their letter and confirming you will be attending on the day and at the time stated. This small courtesy indicates that you are a well-organised, polite person who can make time to supply the personal response in your job hunting.

If you cannot attend an interview, you should telephone the organisation concerned as soon as possible and ask if your interview can be rearranged. However, you should only do this if you definitely cannot attend. In large organisations interviews are normally booked on one specific day, with candidates coming in one after another. If you cannot get to your appointment, there is normally no other time that can be allocated. Nor is it usually possible to see one candidate on a different day, especially if more than one person is interviewing. If at all possible, attend the interview allocated to you; the manager wants to get on with the appointment and will not want to wait.

On no account ring the firm and ask to rearrange your interview, and if they refuse, tell them you can manage to attend at the original time and date after all. Many candidates do this and it gives the impression they don't really want to make the effort to attend but if the firm pushes, they will attend. This is not the best first impression to make and may well be remembered at the interview.

Of course, smaller firms can be much more flexible, particularly where only one interviewer is involved.

Research for the interview

This section can be split into three areas of research:

- Finding out about the company
- Finding out about the job
- Finding out about the interview.

The company

You will need to know something about the organisation which may be offering you a job in the near future. There are different reasons for wanting to do this.

First, you will want to know whether or not the firm has a future, and what the prospects are for a long period of employment with that organisation. As mentioned earlier, opportunities are better with an expanding firm as opposed to one that is contracting. It is quite possible that one branch of a firm could be recruiting new employees unaware that the parent body is in serious financial difficulties and may have to close down in the near future. If a firm is in trouble you need to know that, although you still might want to consider a job.

The second reason for finding out about the organisation is to equip yourself with the information to perform well at an interview. The candidate who knows something about the firm, what its products are, who the main customers are, will have a much better interview than the candidate who just turns up. In addition, because of the knowledge you have gained, you will approach the interview with confidence. You will be well prepared.

Therefore, in summary, the type of information to get hold of covers:

- What the firm does
- Its range of products
- Where the main offices are
- Where the factories and warehouses are
- How big it is
- How many people work there
- Its reputation
- Its current plans and problems.

There are several potential sources of information regarding an organisation. The first is the letter asking you to attend the interview. If it is on the firm's headed paper, does it list any board members, other factories, offices, or points of contact? Additionally, some organisations will send out publicity material with their letters and in that event you should ensure that you know every detail of their material.

The next area to examine is the advertisement. Do not ignore it, as it may tell you a lot about the company. Often advertisements will make a comment about the company such as whether it is small or large, or if it claims to be an expanding or new company. The specific purpose of the advertisement may be mentioned, such as if it tells you they are recruiting people because of new orders or a new product. All the clues in the advertisement should be examined. Try to get a feel for the way the company views itself.

If, after you have read the material, you have any questions, make a note of them and ask about them at the interview. This will show the interviewers that you have thoroughly read their material and thought about what you have been told.

These first two sources of information are, however, open to all candidates. We would expect every sensible candidate to arrive for the interview having absorbed that information. That leaves you with the problem of how to ensure that you have more information about the firm than other candidates. There are other sources of information about companies and these are discussed below.

Friends and relatives

Potential sources of information, which we have discussed earlier, are friends and relatives. You may know someone who works in the company, who could provide chapter and verse regarding the firm. Quite often we have interviewed applicants who have relatives working for our company and time after time the candidates have not tapped this source of information. It is either laziness, lack of thought or lack of effort. Whatever the reason, they are not the type of person that we want to employ. If you know someone who works there, either a relative, friend or neighbour, go and knock on their door and ask for at least half an hour of their time for a briefing on the firm.

The local library

Another source of information, particularly about large organisations, is the local reference library. Here you may be able to find copies of company accounts. Even if it is a small firm you should make sure you look through one or two issues of the relevant trade magazine, then during the interview you can ask if the recent changes to, say, food hygiene legislation, or whatever, that were recently introduced will affect the firm or whether they are worried about the lack of trained fitters, both topics that you might have highlighted in the trade journals. Smaller companies are more difficult to research, but you could try ringing the local Chamber of Commerce.

The organisation

The avenue with most potential is the organisation itself. If you can make a preliminary visit as described below you could ask for any publicity material about the firm, perhaps a catalogue of their products, a copy of the annual report, a copy of their staff magazine etc.

Alternatively, if the firm has showrooms or shops, pay one a visit. Try to chat to the staff and explain you have an interview in the near future, could they provide any information? If you are lucky, a helpful assistant may be able to provide some very useful material. If you do not have the time to carry out all these visits, ring up and ask the public relations department or personnel department, if they have one, to send you some details. However, you should make sure you leave sufficient time before the interview to receive the information and that the department concerned knows the reason for your request and your deadline.

At the end of your research you should have a feel for the industry, a knowledge of the company and an awareness of the problems and topical issues facing that market sector. If you have that awareness at your fingertips, you will be seen as a much more able, confident and knowledgeable candidate and you will approach the matter with more confidence in your own ability to handle the interview and the questions. If you have that confidence, the interview will flow well, you will enjoy it and present a better impression of yourself.

Research for the job

Many of the sources listed above will provide information regarding the job. In particular, look again at the advertisement; it should provide a list of duties and responsibilities. Instead of just reading it, make a list of all of the job-related items mentioned. This will be important later when we start thinking of what areas the interviewers will be asking questions about. Look again at our earlier section on how to read and understand advertisements (page 57).

The firm may send you a job specification with your interview letter. This is a comprehensive list of the tasks involved in the job and should provide all the information you require about it. If you are sent one, make sure you know it thoroughly before the interview and make a note of any areas about which you require clarification.

Finding out about the interview

In the details regarding the interview you will have been given a venue, a date and a time to attend. It is vitally important that you get to the interview on time, on the correct date, at the right place. Often interviewers have been kept waiting by a candidate who didn't think the bus trip took so long, didn't realise it was so far from the station, couldn't get parked etc. If you cannot arrive on time for your interview, what chance is there that you will ever attend work on a regular and consistent basis? You cannot do yourself justice if you arrive breathless and in general disarray having had to run all the way from the bus stop because you were put off at the wrong stop. You will spend the first ten minutes of the interview trying to get your breath back and straighten your hair!

A better course of action would be to carry out a dry run. The first working day before the interview set out at the same time as you would for the interview, get the same bus or train and make sure you can find the correct entrance, reception area or office that you have to find the following day. If on the dry run you cannot get there with time to spare, adjust your timing accordingly. Always make sure you arrive at least 20 minutes before your interview time. This gives you time to settle down and compose yourself.

Waiting for your turn

If you are sitting in the outer office, you may be able to chat to the receptionist who can give some useful advice about the company. Surprisingly, a number of candidates do not attend for interviews nor do they bother to ring up and let the firm know they will not be attending. Or, alternatively, not having carried out a dry run, they are late. This leaves the interviewers sitting around waiting, not knowing if the candidate is attending or not.

On a number of occasions we have rung reception and asked, for example, to see the 10.30 candidate only to be told he has not arrived, but Mr Jones is here for his 10.50 interview. We can either see Mr Jones straight away or wait a little longer for the 10.30 candidate. Either way, when Mr Jones enters for his interview he is in a much stronger position than the candidate who was late.

Even if the candidate has a good reason for being late it often sounds like an excuse. He should have planned better. If we listen to the first few minutes of Mr Jones's interview, we can see what a good impression he has created from the start and how he keeps improving:

> 'Come in Mr Jones. Sorry to keep you waiting, but as I'm sure you heard, the previous candidate turned up late and kept us all waiting. My timetable is now 20 minutes behind schedule.'
>
> (It is very unlikely the 10.30 candidate will get the job.)
>
> 'You must be very keen, Mr Jones. My secretary tells me you were here well before your interview time.'
>
> 'Yes, Mr Smith (our candidate has remembered the interviewer's name), I am very keen on this job and I like to be punctual for appointments.'
>
> 'Well at least you found us all right; the other chap says he spent 20 minutes trying to find us, but to be fair to him I suppose this industrial estate could do with some more signposts.'
>
> 'Yes. I wasn't sure of my way round so I came through yesterday to check my bearings. Anyway, the time waiting wasn't wasted, your secretary gave me a coffee and told me a little about the firm.'

On Mr Jones's interview so far he seems well on the way to getting the job. He has shown:

- He is punctual
- He plans ahead
- He is keen about the job
- He is prepared to make a lot of effort to get the job
- He uses his spare time waiting to do some last minute research.

In the first few minutes he has made an excellent first impression and all because he carried out a dry run, unlike the other candidate.

Things might not go so well for you as they did for Mr Jones, but most interviewers will ask at the start of the interview if you had any difficulty finding the place, travelling etc. You can then slip into your answer the fact that you did a dry run. You then start the interview with a credit for keenness and preparation.

Most interviewers will ask what you know about the firm and/or the job. At that point tell them what you know and tell them of all the effort you put into finding the information. Again, you will be credited with the effort and you will be able to talk knowledgeably in answer to that question. Contrast your response with the candidates who confess that they know nothing about the place or the job. The following answers do nothing for the candidate's chances nor do they help the interview develop into a natural conversation:

'You make dresses and things, don't you?'

'Well, I've seen your vans around town.'

Be prepared and be well briefed.

Questions you might be asked

The next stage we need to give some thought to is in which areas the interviewers will want to ask questions. The first source of information on this will be the advertisement. Once again, sit down with a sheet of paper and a pen and look at the advertisement in detail.

Let's start with the job title, as this should normally give some idea of the range of duties and responsibilities. For example, the job title 'Storeman'. Try thinking of some experience that you have had with a storeman doing his job. It may be that you have had to go to a warehouse to pick up some flatpack furniture or gone to the stores section of a large garage to buy some spare parts for your car. If you have done this, try to imagine such an occasion. Now start thinking what would make the task easier for you, the customer, what would make you say at the end of the transaction, 'He was a good storeman'. If you start with a blank piece of paper, just put down anything that comes into your mind, no matter if it seems far-fetched. Before looking at our list try the exercise yourself and then compare your answers with ours.

We thought we would look for the following points:

- Was he helpful, particularly if we did not know exactly what we wanted?
- Did he take the time and trouble to explain if there was more than one suitable item we could buy?
- If the item was heavy did he help us to load it on to the car?
- Was he cheerful and friendly or grumpy and morose?
- Did we feel as though he was pleased to see us or were we a nuisance interrupting his peaceful day?
- Did he know where the item was and find it quickly? Did we have to stand in a queue while he chatted to workmates?
- Did he charge the right price and give the right change?

The items could go on, but even from that short list you should get a picture of the type of person you want for a storeman and the type you do not want. Most of the qualities relate to the personality of the storeman as opposed to any natural or acquired skills. After making a list like that you should know what the interviewers will be looking for from the customer's point of view.

We can make a similar list from the manager's viewpoint. Again, what qualities would you look for in a storeman if you were the manager? Make your list before you look at ours.

We thought we would look for the following points, which cover what we wanted:

- Someone honest so that stock does not disappear
- Someone who kept the customers happy; someone with all the qualities listed above by the customers
- Someone who could handle money if the customers paid in cash or with plastic or keep the paperwork in order if people handed in dockets for stores issued
- Someone reliable with good attendance because, if the stores are not open every single day, we cannot sell our stock
- Someone prepared to work some overtime and some weekends to do stockchecking.

How does your list compare with ours?

You should now go through the rest of the advertisement making a full list of those qualities and attributes you think you would look for if you were interviewing for the job and you had to appoint someone. Imagine it's your own business and if you make a wrong appointment the loss of profits comes out of your own pocket. What type of questions would you ask the candidates?

Make a list.

Emphasise your qualities for the job

You should now have two lists of the qualities that the ideal candidate should have: one from the customer's point of view and one from the manager's. If you followed our earlier advice, you will have structured your application to stress the importance of your strengths and minimise your weaknesses. Go through the list of qualities required for the job for which you will be interviewed and write down whether you have those qualities or not. When you have finished, go back to the ones marked 'No' and think again. Are you sure that what you think is a weakness cannot be examined in a different light as a strength? Look again at the earlier work we did on strengths and weaknesses; be positive about your strengths. Ask an honest friend if he or she thinks you are weak in that area. Possibly you will have changed some of those negative answers to positive ones.

Check again those few you still have marked 'No'. How will you deal with them in an interview? A good interviewer will ask questions on those areas.

Let's take an example. You are worried because you have no previous experience of this type of work and you think most other candidates may have had experience.

A question might be posed:

> 'I see from your application form you have no previous experience of this type of work. Will that not be a drawback?'
>
> 'No, I don't think so. If you look at my job history to date I think you'll agree I have tried different areas of work and I've always found I pick up things very quickly. Also it means I will not have any preconceived ideas of how the job should be done, so when I get to the training mentioned in your advertisement I'll be following your procedures and techniques, rather than something I've learned somewhere else.'

You should go through each area in which you feel slightly weak and try to work out a strategy for dealing with any questions in that area.

As a last resort, if you cannot think of a sound answer, be honest and say:

> 'Yes, I appreciate that is an area in which I'll need some help, although I'm fairly happy with my abilities in the other areas of the job. However, as long as I recognise that weakness I can do something about it, like getting some training or asking for some initial guidance from my supervisor. I think the greatest danger in any new job is thinking you can do all parts of the job and rushing ahead making mistakes all the time.'

Hopefully, we have dealt with any last few weaknesses that were unresolved so we can now look at the longer list of how you match up to the job. Look at your list and that should give you some confidence. If you were on the interview panel, what type of questions would you ask each candidate to see if they had the necessary qualities that you want? Make a list of two or three questions you would ask for each quality.

You now should have a list of the questions you will be asked during the interview. The exact phrases may change but the areas of interest for the interviewers should be the same. So now you can start working out a very rough sketch of how you will answer each question. You know what the interviewer is looking for, you know how far you match up to what is required, so there should be no problem.

The only piece of advice we would give you is to try to provide some proof to support what you are saying you can do. Some interviewers give quite clear signals of what should be the 'right' answer to a question. For example:

> 'We need someone reliable and punctual to open the stores every day at 8.30. Are you reliable and punctual?'

It should come as no surprise that most candidates answer 'Yes' although one or two may answer 'No'. They are either very honest or they do not want the job. Unfortunately, the result is that at the end of the day the interviewer is left with ten candidates who all said they were punctual and reliable, and as the employer probably asked similar leading questions on all other areas of interest, he or she cannot tell who was the best candidate. When this happens the candidate who wants the job has to do some work to make up for poor interviewing skills. Every time you are asked about your abilities, try to support your answer with an example. For instance:

> 'Yes, I'm punctual and reliable. In my last job I was never late and was only off once in eight years and that was because of a broken wrist which happened at work.'

> 'Yes, there is no problem about getting up in the morning and being here on time; my wife starts work half an hour before I do and I have to drop her off on the way in, so if anything I'll be here early.'

Another example would be to respond with a 'Yes' to the question: 'Are you good with your hands?', but you could also respond with an example:

> 'Yes, in fact I recently installed fitted wardrobes at home, starting just from the raw materials. I'm always doing things round the house.'

Avoid, if at all possible, 'Yes' or 'No' answers. If you can elaborate on the point you want to make, without boring the interviewers, then do so. Your task at the interview is to prove to the interviewer that you can do the job and to convince him or her that you are the best person for the job.

Think – what does the interviewer want?

One problem when interviewing is that a number of the candidates could actually do the job, so the interviewer normally looks for the candidate with the best attitude to work and the most commitment to the organisation. The worst thing a candidate can do is to give the impression that this is just another job that they would be quite happy to accept. You must convince the panel that if employed at this firm you would give your very best. Interviewers can appoint any number of average people who are half committed to the organisation. The difficulty is to appoint someone who will make an outstanding contribution to the firm.

The other problem facing interviewers is that, although normally the person appointed will be working with a more experienced person, there is a chance that the more experienced person could be absent for a time, perhaps off ill or on holiday or just out to lunch. Therefore, during most interviews candidates will be questioned on what they would do if they were alone in the office and a problem arose with no one else to give advice. Often the answers to questions of that nature will decide which candidate is appointed. The thing to do with that type of question is to think through the type of work you will be doing before the interview and try to think yourself into a few problem areas. Quite often there is no right answer to these questions but the panel wants to see if you can spot the danger areas involved in a particular type of work. Here is one example which we might ask of an applicant for a job as a clerk in a wages department.

Question:

'What would you do if you answered the phone one day and the person calling said they were from the New Tyne Building Society and they want details of Joe Smith's earnings so they could give him a mortgage?'

Answer:

'Well, I'd check with my supervisor to see if it was in order to release the information.'

Question:

'Unfortunately, everyone else is at lunch, you are the only

one in and the building society wants an answer straight away as Mr Smith might lose a house he wants to buy if he doesn't confirm today that he can have his mortgage.'

Answer:

'I still would not be happy to give out confidential details of someone's earnings. I don't even know if it is the building society on the telephone. Also, I would want someone to check the figures so I would have to wait for someone to come back. Therefore, I would offer to check with the supervisor as soon as she came back from lunch and ring them back as quickly as possible this afternoon. I would ask to whom I was speaking and their section or department. In the meantime I could be getting the figures out and checking the building society's telephone number in the directory so I'm sure I know who I'm ringing. That way there would be very little delay as I'm sure the supervisor will not be away that long.'

The process of the question was that the initial situation was set out by the interviewer and the candidate first tried the most obvious route out of the situation by referring the problem to someone with more knowledge and experience. This is what most people would do in the work situation when faced with a problem they feel is beyond their training and experience. However, the interviewer has decided to press this candidate so he or she then brings in some more information which forces a decision. This candidate has taken our advice and thought about the important elements in working in a wages department, and decided that confidentiality is one of the most important items in dealing with other people's pay; he or she therefore knows that any of these 'What if' questions should be answered with that factor in mind. Also, speed and accuracy are important: people want their pay when it's due to them and they want it correct. So, in the answer the candidate makes the point that the figures would be ready so the supervisor could check them and could then ring the building society straight away.

Would you have dealt with that question as well as that candidate?

You would have if you had taken time before the interview to think through what you thought were the important parts of the job. Remember the lists we made out before; they would have given you all the key elements of the job.

Why not ask a friend to interview you for 20 minutes and run through the type of questions you may be asked?

Preparing your interview questions

At some time during the interview it is normal practice to ask the candidates if they have any questions they would like to ask the interviewers. This is normally done at the end of the interview and many candidates, realising that the interview is almost over, say they have no questions so they can get out as soon as possible. The other natural reaction is for your mind to go blank so you cannot think of any of the points you wanted to raise.

The solution to both these problems is to write down two or three questions before the interview and to have your piece of paper ready when the time comes. Introduce the subject with a smile: 'In case my mind were to go blank at this point I took the precaution of writing some notes beforehand.'

Ask whatever questions you are interested in but do not only ask about the pay and holidays. Candidates who concentrate on these aspects appear greedy and only interested in that side of the job. Ask about the firm, where you will be working if you get the job, if there are opportunities for further training etc.

If you don't want to ask any questions, you can always fall back on the phrase: 'I had some questions but I think you've answered them all during the interview.'

The other thing to avoid is prolonging the interview past the point at which the interviewer wishes to finish. That's why we advise only two or three questions. Many candidates ask too many questions ignoring the clear hints from the interviewers that they have to see other candidates.

Do not talk too much or overstay your welcome.

Dress for the interview

It is surprising how often a candidate's appearance will let them down. Having spent the time and effort getting this far, do not throw it all away by not taking enough care with your appearance.

The appropriate dress will vary with the type of job for which you are applying. The image is important and must support the verbal message that you are sending during the interview.

As a general rule, all office jobs and jobs where you will be required to meet the public warrant a suit and tie for the men and a smart outfit for the women. At least for the interview a dress or skirt is preferable for women and on no account should jeans be worn. For manual jobs a shirt and tie gives a good impression as many people still work on the basis 'smart appearance, smart job'.

Whatever you decide to wear should be clean and pressed. Shoes should be shining and you should be clean and tidy with hair brushed.

Preparation on your appearance should be carried out the night before the interview or earlier, but there are some other preparations to make. You should take most of the following items to your interview, preferably in a briefcase for an office job or an attaché case for other jobs:

- Your letter inviting you for the interview
- Your certificates in respect of your principal qualifications
- Any references you have
- Your CV or copy application form
- Your job-hunt diary and letters log
- Your Youth Training log book (if you have one)
- Anything the firm has asked for in the letter
- Your list of questions to ask.

Whether or not you have an early night before the interview depends on the type of person you are. If an early night means you will wake up refreshed and on top of the world then have one. If you will lie awake worrying about the interview and get less sleep than normal, don't bother.

Checklist for success

- Read the advertisement and any letter from the company carefully
- Learn the names and job titles of the people on the panel
- Make every effort to attend at the time and on the date requested
- Research the company, the job and the interview, *be prepared*
- Carry out a dry run
- Be early
- Think about the questions that will be asked
- Think about your answers
- Give examples of your qualities
- Think of the questions you want to ask
- Stress your strengths.

Chapter 6

The Interview

At the interview

If you have followed the advice given in previous chapters, you should approach the interview confident that you can deal with it in a manner which should ensure that you will be offered the job. However, if you still have some doubts about your ability and about the forthcoming interview, don't worry too much. It is natural to be a little nervous. In fact, some nervousness may well be of assistance. This will be an aid to help you to key yourself up to give your best during the interview. Remember, you normally have half to three-quarters of an hour to convince the interviewer that you are the best person for the job. Don't worry:

- You are well prepared
- You are aware of what may be asked
- You have done all the preparation that we have suggested.

Be observant

When you arrive for the interview you will normally be asked to wait in a reception area. As mentioned in the last chapter, use this time to your advantage. Talk to the receptionist, if there is one, read any promotional literature lying about, or just sit and watch the comings and goings. Try to get a feel for how the organisation works. Are people cheerful, greeting each other by first names, or is it more formal? This type of information will give you some indication of how to react during the interview. Do not forget to be polite and pleasant to the receptionist. Try and strike up a conversation. That person may be a source of information and interviewers may well ask the receptionist's opinion of each candidate.

In the waiting room, run through the questions you think you will be asked and the answers that you will provide. Before the interview you should have spent some time getting up to date on current affairs, particularly any that affect the firm or industry for which you are applying. Re-read the letter that was sent asking you to come for interview. Marshall your facts; get yourself organised. Nobody attempts to run a race without warming up first. You should do this for a mental race as well. Key yourself up; mentally warm up.

Try to relax

If there are other candidates waiting, don't let their confident conversation worry you. Many people who appear confident do so only to cover their nervousness. Remember, if you have followed our earlier advice you will be well prepared and there should be no hidden surprises in the interview.

It should help you to remember that everyone is nervous at an interview. Also you can help yourself by simple relaxation techniques: calmly and slowly breathing in and out is the easiest and most effective. Try placing your hands on your knees; touch thumb and index finger on each hand lightly and tell each part of your body to relax; start with your feet and work up. While doing this breathe in and out deeply. You may try and relax by smoking but this is inadvisable these days as others may take offence. Chewing gum or sweets may be tempting but we would hope that nobody needs to be told that candidates should not enter the interview chewing; nor should they chew during the interview.

Before entering the interview, pause for a moment and remember that all your preparation means that:

- You are smartly and comfortably dressed
- You have done your research
- You have a good idea what you might be asked
- You have a good idea of your answers.

There is nothing to be concerned about, just go in and make sure you get the job!

Do not be negative

Never go into an interview with a negative outlook. The job has been promised to someone else or they never employ people over 30 etc. That attitude will show through in your performance in the interview. The interviewers will notice you have a chip on your shoulder or that you are half-hearted about the job, therefore it is unlikely that you will be appointed. If that happens, you will think your original idea was right: the job had been promised to someone; they never do employ people over 30. What has actually happened is you have proved your own idea, but it is because of your own attitude.

Similarly, some school leavers give the impression of a lack of interest in the job for which they are applying. People have told them how hard it is to get work so to avoid a big disappointment they play down the importance of the job. Interviewers often complain that school leavers could do the job but they seem to lack get up and go. A school leaver who went into an interview with enthusiasm and commitment to that job would stand an excellent chance of being appointed.

Be yourself and sell yourself

Remember, in an interview, just be yourself. That's what they expect to see. Don't try to be something that you are not, and certainly don't try to change your voice or your accent. As soon as you come under any sort of pressure your accent will slip back. Even if you can maintain a false image throughout the interview and you are subsequently offered the job, could you maintain that false image for the rest of the time you work there?

Having entered the room, wait to be asked to sit down and when you do sit down, try not to move the chair. Some candidates have a habit of moving the chair very close to the interviewer thinking perhaps that this closeness will help to build up rapport. What normally happens then is that the interviewer shrinks back and moves his or her chair further back.

Interviewing techniques

Interviewing techniques vary. In larger organisations the usual situation will be two or three interviewers. That may seem unfair as you are on your own but, as a long-term commitment is being made, the company may wish to involve different departments (perhaps personnel and the department in which you will be employed) and also different levels of management (perhaps the departmental manager and the immediate supervisor). Of course, in a smaller company where such complexity does not exist, one, and occasionally two, people interviewing is normal.

You may find that the interviewer(s) is/are sitting behind a desk with you in front of the desk and this formal situation is still very popular. However, some interviewers think that the desk acts as a barrier to communications. There is a tendency now for interviewers perhaps not even to face the candidate but to sit beside him/her. The idea here is to move away from the confrontation of staring at each other and to try to develop the interview into a pleasant discussion. Whichever system is used, the interviewer eventually has to make the decision to select a candidate. So, while all these moves to put the candidate at their ease are quite helpful, remember this is an important occasion for you.

Once you have settled yourself on your chair, try not to fidget. If you have a habit of waving your arms around, try to stop. Clasp your hands in your lap in a relaxed manner and keep them there.

Some interviewers may ask if you wish to smoke during the interview and may even offer you a cigarette. Our advice is: don't smoke even when asked. The best thing to do is to get the interview out of the way and then have a cigarette as soon as you leave the premises. You will probably enjoy it more after the interview and you don't run the risk of offending a non-smoker on the interviewing panel. Also, there is an increasing number of employers who do not allow smoking at work. If that is the case, they will tell you.

Similarly, some candidates may be offered a cup of coffee. Our advice would be to decline the offer, as the coffee normally acts as a distraction to your concentration. If there are three people interviewing, two of them will be drinking their coffee while the third one asks you questions. The problem with you drinking coffee is that you should be constantly thinking, working and talking throughout the interview, and there is nothing more offputting for candidates than to be asked another question just as they are getting the cup to their lips. Most candidates we have seen do not manage to finish their cup of coffee, and if you are nervous, you may even knock the cup over.

The most informative type of interview would be to let the candidates carry out the job itself to see how they perform. In most instances this is not practical so the interviewer attempts – normally through questions and answers – to assess each candidate's suitability for the job. So bear in mind that the prospective employer is trying to build up an accurate picture of the candidate doing that job all through the interview. This may help to predict and explain some of the questions you will be asked.

Panel interviews are easier from the interviewer's point of view because, believe it or not, interviewing candidates is quite a difficult task. After asking a question, the interviewer is required to listen closely to the answer, while deciding on the next question to ask and yet still be flexible enough to pick up any interesting points or inconsistencies from previous questions. With more than one interviewer, the sharing of the tasks can assist the process, whereas a single interviewer can be so involved with moving the interview through the various necessary stages, he or she can miss some interesting areas of discussion. So in a panel interview you may find an interviewer coming back to you regarding your answer to an earlier question, for example:

> 'You mentioned earlier in answer to one of my colleague's questions that you had supervisory experience at one of your previous jobs. As you are aware the job you have applied for involves supervision and I would be interested to hear more about this aspect of your previous experience.'

There is nothing sinister in this follow-up question. The interviewer seems to feel that his or her colleague did not get all the information on the candidate's strength in this area and is giving the candidate a further opportunity to stress this particular strength.

The extreme version of the panel interview is the interview board, which can consist of more than ten interviewers. How one candidate is expected to relate to so many people in a 30-minute interview is difficult to imagine, but the technique is still used, and candidates who come across it can only console themselves with the knowledge that conditions are the same for all.

The pattern of the interview

Interviews generally follow a set pattern, particularly if the interviewers are trained and competent. The following is a typical pattern:

- Candidate enters the room
- Introductions
- Opening pleasantries
- Information given
- Checking facts
- Assessing abilities
- Assessing personality

- Assessing motivation
- Candidate asks questions
- Candidate is informed of next stage of the process and when the outcome will be announced
- Interview concluded and candidate leaves the room

Always look at the interviewer

During the interview do not use the interviewer's first names even if he or she uses yours. If possible, refer to the interviewers by their titles and surnames, eg Mr Jones, as this tends to build up rapport and confirm respect. Listen to what is being said and pay attention. You should always look at the interviewer even if you are nervous. Nothing is worse than a candidate who constantly stares around the room, looks out of the window, gazes at the floor or never looks at the interviewer.

Do not try to be humble, docile or to agree with the interviewer all the time. Sometimes you will be given questions to provoke you to disagree and to advance your own point of view. After all, when you are doing the job there will be times when you will need to make up your own mind, and the interviewer is interested in your own views. As long as you have thought through your views and they are logical and consistent, they are as acceptable as anyone else's. Be yourself and state your own mind but do not try to win an argument with the interviewer. You will not be thanked even if (and probably especially if) you are right.

Watch the interviewers for non-verbal indications of their feelings. If they are looking round the room and not at you, or alternatively you see them glancing at a clock or tapping their fingers, you may be talking too much and losing their interest, or the interviews may be running late. Conversely, if your answers are punctuated by nodding and agreement with you, you are being encouraged to talk. We all use this body language to give signals, so try to be aware of the 'silent conversation'.

The interviewer may take notes

The interviewer may well take notes during the interview and you should not concern yourself with this. After interviewing constantly for a day or longer, it is extremely difficult to remember which candidates said what, or indeed what each candidate looked like. Interviewers often use notes to supplement their memory, while some firms take candidates' photographs and this aspect of the interview should not concern you. Do not become worried if, after having difficulty with a particular question, an interviewer hurriedly writes a note. It could have nothing to do with your answer, and anyway there are no right or wrong answers in an interview, there are only opinions.

Most professional interviewers use some kind of marking chart to assist in systematically judging and comparing different candidates. The systems in use, and the qualities assessed, may vary but the basic principles are the same: to try to use a common yardstick to assess all candidates. A system used in one large organisation is shown in the figure opposite.

Looking at the scheme should give you some idea of why the interviewer asks certain questions, for instance he or she could be trying to find out about your relevant experience, or your qualifications. Before each interview look at the scheme and decide how you would mark your own performance in each area; the marks should all be in either the excellent or above average category. If they are not, do something to improve them. Do the same thing after each interview but ask yourself whether or not you demonstrated to the interviewer your full experience and potential under each heading. If you did not, then make sure you improve for your next interview.

Let the panel finish asking a question

Always let the panel (or interviewer) finish asking a question before you rush in to answer it. There is a tendency to start answering quickly, probably as a sign of relief that you know the answer. Please let the question be asked and do not interrupt. Use the time to listen to his or her question and any additional information he or she is supplying.

You may wish to pause for a fraction of a second before answering; this allows you to collect your thoughts and to work out exactly what you want to say to the panel. It also, correctly, gives the impression of thoughtfulness.

Answer the question asked

The other point to watch is to make sure you answer the question you have been asked. That may seem obvious, but many candidates either mishear or misunderstand the question and

	Excellent	Above average	Accept-able	Doubtful	Unaccept-able
Appearance/speech					
Drive/enthusiasm					
Intellect/imagination					
Education/qualifications					
Knowledge of job					
Relevant experience					

ramble off into areas which have no relevance to what the interviewer asked. If you do not know the answer to a question, have an intelligent guess. If you are totally lost, ask the panel to repeat the question or amplify it for you; they will normally rephrase it and provide you with more information.

Do not be afraid of short silences

Do not be afraid of short silences in interviews and do not rush in to fill them. Pauses in conversation are quite natural, giving time for speakers to collect their thoughts and progress logically on to the next subject.

'Blanking out'

One thing that often happens to candidates is that they dry up while giving an answer. A fairly simple question can sometimes lead to a candidate's mind 'blanking out'. Don't worry about this. This often happens to interviewers who can forget what the next question should be. If it happens to you, explain to the panel what has occurred:

> 'I'm sorry my mind's gone blank. Could we move to another question?'
>
> 'Sorry I just can't think of an answer to that. Could we come back to it?'

Don't become over-concerned about this if it happens. Interviewers have been through the situation before and they know that people dry up. It will not be held against you.

Be positive

We have discussed previously the nature of possible questions and the type of answers you should provide, but here we are concerned with candidates' attitudes. From the questions that you will be asked at the interview there are several types of answer that you should avoid. Be positive when answering questions, in your attitude to the interview and your approach to the job. Remember, anything is possible if you have the enthusiasm and the energy to carry it through. As sales people say: 'There are no obstacles, only opportunities.'

Each new challenge is a chance to learn, to try new solutions and to find out a little more about your abilities. How you are perceived will depend not so much on what you say in answer to a question but on how you say it. Therefore, in all your answers, be positive, be enthusiastic and you will be successful.

Remember to respond in a positive manner to any questions which relate to how you will solve any problems which may arise in your new job. When you start a new job you will find problems and difficulties, and interviewers are interested in how applicants plan to deal with those problems. A typical question may be as follows:

> 'You are no doubt aware, Mr Jones, that there are a number of internal candidates for this post. How will you deal with any resentment you might experience from those unsuccessful candidates, bearing in mind you would be their new manager?'
>
> 'Well, I think I can understand their disappointment at not being promoted, but I would tackle the problem by having a word with them. They all had a fair opportunity to apply for the job and state their case. The interviewer decided, all things considered, to appoint me. It's no use harbouring a grudge as no matter who was successful we still have to get on with the job in hand. If they were genuine about their interest in promotion, I would imagine they are committed to doing a good job, so I would try to appeal to that instinct and get the team working together as soon as possible.

Be committed to this job, be enthusiastic and impress upon the panel exactly why you consciously decided to apply for the job and why you really want to work for their organisation.

Do not criticise your previous or present employer

You should avoid criticising your teacher, previous employer, supervisor or colleagues. Many people attend interviews not particularly interested in the job for which they are applying but totally committed to getting away from their current job which they dislike. The following phrases do not impress an interviewer:

'I do not get on with my current supervisor.'
'I just want to get out of my current job.'
'My previous manager was very badly organised and could not the manage the office properly. I made all the decisions and got things done.'

We know of candidates who were very well qualified for jobs but came to the interview more interested in talking about what was wrong with their current manager, organisation or job so that the interviewers lost interest in the candidate. Managers have commented:

'The last candidate could certainly have done the job and probably was the best person for the job but the way he spoke about his current manager shows he has no loyalty. I would be scared stiff he would be talking about me, behind my back, within a month or two. We will appoint the other candidate.'

You can tell the interviewer why you are looking for a change or why you left a job, but do not turn it into a personal attack on others. You will only be seen as bitter and disloyal. Give the facts and let them draw any necessary conclusions. If you are too strident, it may be you who comes across as difficult to work with.

When answering questions, be polite; do not swear and do not 'umm' and 'ahh'.

Try to expand your answers

Sometimes interviewers might come to the interviews not very well prepared. A good panel will have read your application form and have questions prepared; however, others might not be that well prepared and may decide to conduct an ad hoc interview. This is unprofessional and is not conducive to a good set of interviews. However, you as the candidate will have to cope with this problem. Try to expand your answers to their questions; try to develop the interview from short questions and answers into a pleasant conversation.

Handling a noisy or interrupted interview

The other aspect of a bad interview that you may have to cope with is if the interviewer has not made the necessary preparations to provide a quiet, undisturbed interview location. Good interviews will be carried out in a room where telephones will not ring and interruptions from other members of the organisation or background noise is avoided. However, this may not always happen and if you are interviewed in a situation where the secretary is constantly interrupting with messages or where the telephone is constantly ringing during your interview, while this is particularly unprofessional conduct on the interviewer's part, you must try to maintain the natural flow of the conversation. Grin and bear these interruptions and ultimately continue to impress the interviewer that a good candidate is available, notwithstanding the interviewer's preoccupation with other matters.

Of course some interruptions are unavoidable and you should be able to deal with these in a confident and relaxed manner. An example of this happened when some interviews for the post of personal secretary to the sale director were being conducted. During the interview the fire alarm sounded and the panel and candidate had to evacuate the building for a fire drill. The candidate, who up to that time had not been seen as the best candidate, came across as able to continue the conversation and make small talk under unusual situations. An ability to deal with an unexpected situation and to talk to two complete strangers was felt an important ability for a private secretary. The candidate was subsequently offered the job. Therefore:

Be prepared for the unexpected.

One point we would make is that whatever the interviewer's conduct, you should always remember that the interviewer decides who gets the job. So you can be kept waiting, the interviewer can be unprepared for the interview and can show his or her bad temper but you, the candidate, should at all times try to remain calm, pleasant and unruffled! Of course, you may wish to reconsider whether you want a job working in such an environment. That decision should only be taken when you have been offered the job.

If, during the interview, there are any topics or areas on which you would like some further information, ask as the topic arises, but do not do this too often as the panel really wants to spend the time getting information from you. Watch for non-verbal signs to gauge whether or not the panel welcomes your questions.

Remember: the interviewer relies on you to give him or her the information he or she needs in order to decide whether to appoint you. What you say is therefore of crucial importance, so stress your strengths and do not dwell on your weakness. Be positive not negative.

There is no need to rush out of the room at the end of the interview, but again, do not overstay your welcome; remember, they have a timetable to keep. Have the confidence to be polite, thank the panel for seeing you and for considering you for the job.

When you leave the interview you should feel that you have done yourself justice, that you had every opportunity to show what qualities and strengths you have to offer. You should also feel that all the information needed to make a decision has been given and that the employer will decide to offer you the job. At the end of the interviewing process you should feel that even if you are not offered the job, it should be through no fault of yours. It will happen that at some interviews there will be a perfect candidate who was just made for the job. If that happens, do not worry. The only time to feel disappointed was if you did not do yourself justice. If that has happened, after all our advice, the only thing to do is to try again and make sure you do better the next time.

Have you had a hard time?

If you think you have had a hard interview where the interviewer throws a lot of difficult questions at you and puts you under a little pressure, do not worry. If a candidate appears to have promise, quite often an employer will increase the difficulty of the questions just to see how capable that candidate really is. Conversely, do not assume that because the interview went well and you seemed to get on well with the interviewers you will get the job. Good interviewers put all the candidates at their ease and make sure the interviews go well. This does not mean they want to appoint all the candidates: they are just doing their job. The only way to know if you have been successful is to wait for the letter offering you the job.

Getting the needle

A further stage on from asking candidates difficult questions is the interviewer who aggressively challenges a candidate regarding previous answers and statements. This needling style of questioning is sometimes used to ascertain how well each candidate can handle pressure which can be present in some jobs, for instance a sales person dealing with an awkward, complaining customer. The aim of the questions is to find out how far the candidate can be pushed before he or she responds aggressively to the interviewer, the basic response by the candidate, therefore, must be to remain calm in the face of this aggression. Pause before responding to the interviewer's challenge; think about his statement; is he being unreasonable? Do not hesitate too long in your reply as the panel may think you lack the ability to think quickly on your feet.

Finally, do not forget that one response - and there comes a time when it should be used on an awkward or aggressive person - is to challenge him. Tell him you think he is being unreasonable in his outlook. If he is playing the part of the awkward customer and you have done everything you can think of to placate him, throw the matter back to him:

> 'Well, I've done my best to help you, and gone a considerable way to meet your demands. I am not sure I can do more to help you.'

Are you promotable?

One further point regarding interviews is that, quite often, all the candidates could do the job for which they are applying. If they cannot, they should not have got past the shortlisting stage and been called in for interview. Therefore, we often look for people who can progress in years to come. You should be aware of this when applying for jobs and prepare for some questions regarding the supervisor's job or regarding more complex situations than will arise in the actual job for which you are applying. One of the school leavers that we interview for an apprenticeship may well be the future managing director of the organisation. As Napoleon said: 'Every French soldier carries in his cartridge pouch the baton of a marshall of France.'

Similarly, every applicant for a job has the chance to progress to the executive suite if he or she wishes and has the ability. Remember, however, you can overdo this and put an employer off if you are considered so ambitious that you would quickly become bored by the job on offer.

After the interview

After the interview there is a temptation to forget everything that occurred during that crucial half an hour or hour, just as we try to blot out of our minds unpleasant events! That is all very well if you are offered the job but an interview is an opportunity to learn as well as a chance to obtain employment. Even if you are offered the first job for which you apply, there will be other interviews in the future, either for promotion or as you seek to change jobs in order to improve your career.

After the interview, sit down with pen and paper and list what went well and what went badly. Keep the lists for future reference, so you do not make the same mistakes again. Have a look at the what-went-badly list and make sure you do not make similar mistakes again. Write down as many of the questions as you can remember and then write down how you dealt with them. Talk the questions and answers over with a friend. Could he or she have dealt with any of the questions in a better way? On reflection, were there any ways you could have stressed your strengths more than you did? Were you negative in any of your attitudes? Do not be too critical; on calm reflection we can always do better, but it is a useful exercise to help you learn for the future. Remember that the experience of this interview can help on future occasions.

Tests and their uses

As mentioned on page 79, the best method of selection for a job would be to let each candidate actually do the job for a period of time to see how they got on. In most cases this is not practical, so some organisations use specially designed tests which, it is claimed, measure specific abilities. The organisation selects which abilities are important for the job in question and then decides which test measures those abilities. For instance, a typing test would be used to select a typist or someone for a job requiring keyboard skills. The results from the test are often used in conjunction with the interview as success in the test usually predicts someone will perform well in the job.

Tests are useful as they can be given to a number of candidates at the same time; they are therefore much quicker and more objective than interviews. The rules of the tests and the questions are exactly the same for each candidate and therefore everyone has the same chance. The person giving the test has detailed instructions to follow and most tests are carefully timed, usually with a stopwatch, to ensure candidates get equal treatment every time the test is used.

Our advice on attending testing sessions is similar to our advice on attending interviews. Get there early, do a dry run to find the place, dress smartly and get there mentally prepared to work hard. Most tests start with some practice questions to get candidates in the swing for what is required. During the practice questions the person giving the test is allowed to explain the instructions and give some guidance. Getting the right answer to the examples is not that important but it is vital that you understand what is required on each question. If you are not happy, ask for help. You will probably be taking the test with other candidates and there is a tendency to feel embarrassed at being the only one to ask, a feeling that everyone else has picked up the instructions. You must overcome that feeling and ask; there will be other people in the room who have not picked it up; do not throw away the chance of a job just because you do not want to appear foolish in front of others. When we come to mark the answers in every testing session we do, at least one candidate has not understood what was required and has, as a result, scored very low marks.

Once the test starts there will normally be a set number of questions to answer in a given time. The time limit is normally quite short so few people finish all the questions; if more time was given most people would finish and get them right. Work as quickly but as accurately as you can; normally the early questions are easier with later questions becoming more difficult. If you cannot answer a question, do not linger too long on it: move on to the next one and, if you have time, you can go back and try again later. Avoid wild guesswork. If you do manage to finish, do not sit looking pleased with yourself. Go back in the time remaining and check your answers: at least one of them will be wrong.

The score you get on a test reflects your ability for the task the test is meant to measure and as such there is no pass or fail score. Your score is measured against scores obtained by a large number of people of similar age and background and you will either be above or below average. The test score should be high in tasks you feel you are good at and low in those subjects you are not. There would be little point in comparing test scores of a clerk and a mechanic on a clerical aptitude test, unless of course it was to find out if they were potentially able to switch jobs.

Preliminary interviews

Sometimes, if a job is particularly hard to fill or if there is a large number of candidates, an organisation will carry out preliminary interviews to shortlist candidates for a final interview. This will be a first sieve of candidates whose applications look reasonable based on the forms provided. If this happens to you, you should deal with it as a normal interview but it will probably be shorter and the questions less searching. Concentrate on being shortlisted. You will probably receive less information about the job than normal as full details will be provided at the final interview. Remember, this is a further hurdle and more information will be requested and supplied at the final interview.

Negotiating salary

Would you accept the job if it was offered? Some firms ask candidates during the interview what salary they are hoping to obtain. This is always a difficult point because you want to get the maximum rate for the job but do not want to price yourself out of the market. Be realistic. Before the interview make some enquiries of any contracts in similar trades; work out how much you need to live on; decide whether or not you are looking for an increase on your previous earnings. If possible, delay the decision until you know whether or not the firm wants to offer you the job; if they do, you are in a much stronger bargaining position. Above all, do not lose the job by being greedy – be realistic. Get the job first and then weigh up the chances of a pay rise after you have been there a while.

One way to handle this problem is to say something like, 'I naturally want to earn as much as my background and experience will permit. In my last job (where relevant) I made £000 per week/year. However, the most important point for me is the job and the people I work with. If I am the person you want, and I am sure I am right for this job, then I believe you will make me a reasonable offer.' You could then add, 'What figure do you have in mind?'

The problem is thus not avoided but the wrong signals are not given.

Checklist for success

- Get there early and be observant while waiting
- Settle down and relax, use some simple techniques to aid relaxation

- Do not be negative about the interview; be positive and hopeful
- Think of the questions you are likely to be asked
- Think of the stages of the interview and be confident
- Look at the interviewer, not at the floor or elsewhere
- The interviewer is assessing you and may make notes
- Do not interrupt the interviewer
- Answer the question that you have been asked
- Do not criticise previous employers, supervisors or colleagues
- Stay calm if the interviewer tries to needle you
- Review your performance after the interview and see if you can improve next time
- Do not be nervous of tests.

Chapter 7

What is Work Like?

The workplace

Having followed our advice throughout the book you should now be in a position to actually start your job. This chapter will cover some of the terms and conditions you will meet at the workplace. It will concentrate on items which may appear strange to the person new to the world of work, although if you have worked before, you may find you are already knowledgeable. However, work is a different environment from what may have been encountered previously, particularly by the average school leaver.

This chapter is divided into six sections:

- Accepting the job offer
- Your legal position at work
- Terms and conditions
- Money at work
- Variable terms and conditions
- Safety and environment.

Accepting the job offer

If you are offered a job this will either be:

- Verbally at the time
- By telephone afterwards
- By letter.

What we have said before about larger and smaller companies applies. The large, complex organisations will send a detailed package of documents with a formal acceptance paper for you to complete and return. This package may well include other documents such as company rules, grievance procedures, and so on.

In practice, a written acceptance should be made to a written offer. All verbal exchanges can form the basis of a contract between employer and employee, but unless any points are recorded it is difficult to determine in the future what the terms of the offer, and therefore your acceptance, were.

So, even in response to a verbal offer, confirm in writing that you wish to accept the job and indicate when you will start. We set out below the further details you will receive in a contractual statement.

One word of caution: do not give notice to your existing employer (if you have one) or leave school unless you are sure the offer is certain and final. Offers, especially verbal ones, can be withdrawn.

Remember also that any offer may well be subject to a medical examination and taking up references. The apparently silliest items can be a problem here. A minor offence as a juvenile might disbar you; or perhaps slight colour blindness that you have never known about could lead to your failing a medical. Please do not worry, but make sure you know everything is certain before you commit yourself and, say, resign your present job or course.

Finally, do not rush to accept the first offer. Enthusiasm is understandable (and you may be pressed to accept quickly) but the first offer may not be the right one and another may be in the post. Always go home and think about it. A few days' delay will not usually stop you accepting an offer. This applies particularly to school leavers who need to think carefully whether the job offered is what they want. If you make the wrong choice, and want to leave soon, it looks very bad on your CV.

Your legal position at work

When you start work you have a contract of employment with your employer and you should receive a letter of employment or statement of terms and conditions setting out the main details of that contract of employment. However, there are other terms and conditions that are assumed to exist between an employer and employee in the eyes of the law. For instance, an employee is expected to give fair, reasonable, diligent service in exchange for the payment the employer offers.

Although these terms will not be explicitly stated in your letter of employment, they are your contractual obligations. Therefore, your contract of employment covers not just the written letter of employment but also all the implied and unwritten conditions assumed to exist between the employer and the employee. In the event of a dispute between the employer and the employee, this distinction between the two expressions can be important and many employees have found to their cost how wide-ranging implied terms can be.

Letters of appointment and statement of contract

Under existing employment law each employee must be given, within 13 weeks of starting work, a statement of the main terms and conditions appertaining to his or her employment or details of where the information can be found, for instance in a staff handbook. Many organisations issue this letter of employment prior to a new employee starting work. The letter must cover certain items and these are:

- Names of the employer and the employee
- The rate of pay
- Whether payment will be weekly or monthly and how payment will be made
- Any terms and conditions relating to hours of work (including normal working hours)
- Any terms and conditions relating to:
  holidays including bank holidays
  incapacity for work due to sickness or injury
  including any sick pay or pension schemes
- The length of notice of leaving which the employee is obliged to give and entitled to receive or, if the contract is for a fixed term, the date at which the contract expires
- The title of the job which the employee is employed to do.

The terms and conditions explained

The above are the bare legal minimum although many letters of employment cover other areas as well and they can be fairly bulky documents. The following covers these points in more detail.

Names of the employer and the employee

(self-explanatory)

The rate of pay

This could be stated as an annual, monthly, weekly or daily amount, or as an hourly rate. Some organisations retain the differential that staff employees have their pay stated as an annual or monthly amount, whereas a manual worker has pay expressed as a weekly, daily or hourly rate. It can be difficult to define the difference between staff and manual employees, although traditionally staff employees worked in an office while manual workers worked with their hands and contributed to the production of tangible items.

In a large organisation you may have a salary within a stated range which guarantees your progression to a higher salary. The 'salary scale' is a peculiarly British tradition used extensively by the Civil Service, nationalised industries and local authorities. These 'annual increments', as each salary increase is called, are additional to any other general increase in pay scales negotiated with employees and their representatives.

One final point on pay is that you will probably be paid in arrears. That means you will work a week or even a month before you get paid. This can be a problem when you first start work, although if you are in receipt of state benefit there may be provision for you to continue to receive the benefit until your first pay is received. You should check your entitlement with the appropriate government department.

Whether payment will be weekly or monthly

This is covered above but it is worth noticing that under previous legislation, if you were a 'manual' employee and paid weekly, you were entitled to receive the amount due in cash if you so wished. Monthly paid employees did not have that legal entitlement. However, this law has been repealed and employers can now insist on all new starters being paid monthly, and having their salaries paid directly into a bank account. This is an efficient and increasingly popular method.

Any terms and conditions relating to hours of work (including normal working hours)

The hours of work will normally be expressed as so many hours a week or more fully as:

- So many hours a week on certain days
- Starting and finishing time
- And could cover lunch and/or rest periods.

You may, however, be employed on an 'annualised hours'

contract. In this case, there will be variations during weeks or months or across the seasons. In any event, the terms of such an arrangement will be discussed with you.

Flexible working systems which require people to clock in and out have been introduced in some companies. These systems can provide some choice of when you arrive at work, when you leave and how long you take for lunch, and this may be covered in your letter of employment. It should be pointed out that the operation of flexible working hours occurs usually at the discretion of the supervisor or manager. Employees cannot leave if the result would be insufficient cover to deal with the work. This sort of flexible working is used in offices but is not common in retailing or in factories.

In some industrial jobs you may also be required to clock on and clock off at starting and finishing times. This is normally used to check employees' timekeeping and employees who do not observe the correct times may lose money and/or face disciplinary action. This type of clocking on and off is not done to allow flexible working of the type mentioned above.

Any terms and conditions relating to holidays including bank holidays

Your holiday entitlement will vary from one organisation to another, perhaps increasing with your length of service. Most employees will be entitled to the statutory bank holidays, currently eight days a year. If employees are required to work bank holidays, normally there will be provision for extra payment or time off at a different time. Remember, though, that a bank holiday is literally a holiday for banks, not necessarily for everyone else, and even bank staff cannot in law insist on payment, although payment is normal.

As with flexible working hours, the taking of holidays, apart from bank holidays, is normally at the discretion of a supervisor or manager. It is unlikely that a lot of employees can take their holidays at the same time unless, as is the case in some industries, it is traditional to close the entire works so everyone has to take their holidays at the same time.

Whichever system is in operation will affect your ability to take holidays at different times of the year. Schoolteachers, for instance, enjoy a generous holiday entitlement but can only take those holidays at term end or half term.

Any terms and conditions relating to incapacity for work due to sickness or injury including any provision for sick pay

The sick pay offered will vary with each organisation, although there are certain legal minimum entitlements. You will find that the basic benefits are limited and any company benefits may require special conditions such as the provision of medical certificates.

Any terms and conditions relating to pension and pension schemes

The pension and pension scheme will vary with each organisation but will either consist of membership of the state scheme or of the employer's scheme, which must meet certain minimum standards. If it is the employer's own scheme, it will either be contributory or non-contributory. With a contributory scheme the employee will be required to pay a sum from earnings into the scheme, as well as the contribution from the employer. In a non-contributory scheme only the employer makes a contribution.

The latter case will mean the employee will be left with more of his or her earnings but it is also important to check at an early stage what your pension scheme will provide for you. Do not leave it until two or three years before retirement, as by then it will be too late. If you are not happy with the provision made for your retirement, the time to do something about providing for your old age is when you are in your twenties or thirties. An insurance policy at that age to provide money for when you are 60 will not be expensive. However, a similar policy at age 50 will be. If you are young this all sounds irrelevant, but regrettably the years pass quickly.

Any terms and conditions relating to the length of notice of termination

The length of notice which the employee is obliged to give and is entitled to receive or, if the contract is for a fixed term, the date at which the contract expires must be stated.

These details will be set by the organisation subject to certain legal requirements. It should be noted that you cannot suddenly terminate your employment without running the risk of losing some financial benefit and you should study your letter of employment closely before making a decision on resigning. If you wish to leave, please try to ensure you have the certainty of another job. It is easier to find a job if you are already in work as opposed to being unemployed. Having taken all this time, trouble and effort to get a job you should not be in a hurry to throw it away.

The title of the job which the employee is employed to do
The title of the job should give you an indication of the type of duties that you will be expected to undertake and what you would not be expected to do. Therefore, a job title of Typist neatly encapsulates the work involved and, by implication, the person involved would not be expected to rewire office equipment, dig holes in a road etc. However, these days flexibility is the key word, so a typist may also carry out clerical duties, cover reception, deal with customers and so on.

Trade unions
Individual employees, under current legislation, cannot be fairly dismissed for being members of an independent trade union or for proposing to become a member. Employees have the right not to belong to a trade union. A closed shop is an agreement or arrangement between an employer and a trade union or trade unions which requires employees covered by the closed shop agreements to be members of a specified trade union or trade unions. Following changes in legislation, closed shop agreements are now uncommon. In practice, whether you join a trade union will largely depend on the common practice in the place where you work.

Unfair dismissal
This legislation means that an employee cannot be dismissed unfairly after a certain period of employment (currently two years). Normally, an employer is entitled to dismiss an employee if the dismissal is classed as fair in the eyes of the law. The legislation and case law surrounding fair and unfair dismissal is complex and subject to change. Should you find yourself in the position of facing dismissal, you should consult the local office of the Advisory, Conciliation and Arbitration Service (ACAS).

It is worth remembering, though, that this legislation is not in truth a right *not to be dismissed* but a right to *compensation* if you are *unfairly dismissed*. You cannot insist on getting your job back if you are sacked unfairly and a determined employer can simply pay up.

If you have not worked for the employer very long, the payment to you, which is based on service, can be small (normally, a payment of a few hundred pounds). Therefore, the employer has a lot of power and you cannot choose what you say or do at work.

Maternity and paternity rights

Maternity rights can accrue to female employees after a given length of service but some employers offer more than the legal minimum requirements and it is best to check on your firm's local arrangements. Some employers also offer 'family friendly policies' which include benefits such as paternity schemes (ie where the father has a shorter period off work to assist the mother and child) and, again, it is best to check on local arrangements.

Money at work

Most employees have a statutory right to receive from their employers an individual, detailed pay statement at or before the time of payment. This is normally referred to as a payslip and should show your gross earnings, deductions, and the net pay due.

Your rate of pay will normally be agreed between yourself or your representative (often a trade union) and your employer or your employer's representative (often a federation of employers for that industry). Your employer should then pay that amount for each period worked. Most employers also pay a premium rate for any overtime worked outside normal hours of work or they may have a bonus scheme which rewards the efforts of employees above a certain minimum level. These elements should produce the gross pay for the period in question.

Most pay is increased each year by an annual pay settlement which is agreed between an employer and the employee or his or her representatives. This can be a percentage increase of pay or a flat rate increase of so much a week or month, or a combination of both. In hard times certain firms have been known to ask employees to take a pay cut to save jobs.

Taxation

The tax system of this country allows you to earn a set amount of money, depending on your personal circumstances, before you are liable to pay income tax. This allowance is sometimes called free pay, as it is free of tax. Once this amount has been reached, tax is then paid at a set rate on the earnings over that limit. The tax is normally deducted at source by the employer under a system known as Pay As You Earn (PAYE). The income tax collected goes towards providing such items as the National Health Service, roads, defence etc. The amount of free pay and the rates of tax on each level of earnings are normally set each year by the government in the Budget. However, to give an illustration, the tax rates and allowances which applied during 1994–95 were:

Taxable annual earnings	*Tax rate**	*1995–96 taxable annual earnings*
Up to £3,000	20%	Up to £3,200
£3,001–£23,700	25%	£3,201–£24,300
Over £23,700	40%	Above £24,300

*This percentage taken off 'taxable pay', not *all* pay. Taxable pay is pay after personal and other allowances have been deducted. These allowances are tax free.

	Allowance (1995–96)
Single person	£3,525
Married couple	£1,720*

*Relief restricted to 20%.

Other deductions

All employees earning over a certain minimum (set by the government, and announced annually in the Budget) are required to pay National Insurance contributions to go towards hospitals, pensions, sick pay, and other welfare benefits. Again, these will be deducted by the employer at source.

There are other deductions an employer can make from your pay with your permission, eg your trade union subscriptions, savings schemes, contributions to sports and social clubs etc. There are also deductions an employer can make without your consent, eg an attachment of earnings. This could arise if you owe some money and your creditor obtains an attachment of earnings order from a court. If this happens, you will have been notified of the court proceedings at an earlier date and will have had an opportunity to argue the case; also, there are various safeguards on these orders to protect the individual. However, if an employer is presented with this order, he or she has no option but to make the appropriate deductions from the employee's pay.

After these deductions have been taken from your *gross pay* the resulting sum will be shown as the *net pay* and it is this amount that is actually paid to you for the period of employment covered by the payslip.

Managing your money

When you receive your payslip each week or month you should check it closely. Most payroll departments are very accurate but even the best of them can make mistakes; it is best to ensure that *your* pay is correct. Check that the overtime you worked last month has been included, and that your latest tax adjustment has been amended; the five or ten minutes this will take is time well spent.

Many organisations encourage employees to receive their pay directly into their bank accounts as this saves the firm the expense, effort and security problems of paying employees in cash. The employee receives the detailed payslip outlined above which shows how much net pay has been credited to the bank account and the whole transaction is completed in a safe and efficient manner. New employees are often encouraged to open a bank account to allow this process to take place. Most of the large banks will allow someone in employment to open an account with only one reference, which the employer is often pleased to supply. The bank account with a monthly statement of income and expenditure can be a useful aid - if properly used - to the weekly or monthly budgeting process outlined below.

If you are starting work for the first time, you need to consider the amount of money you are receiving each week or month, that is to say your take-home pay. At first your new earnings will probably seem to be a large amount and you may feel that you will have difficulty spending it all. However, we strongly recommend you sit down and work out a weekly or monthly budget by listing all your planned expenditure for the period and then list your income for the period. You should always set aside an amount for each period for unforeseen items such as repairs to your car, a forgotten birthday present, or something as simple as new batteries for your radio. In addition, you should try to put aside a sum of money, no matter how small the amount, as savings to build up a nest egg. Having worked out the difference between your expenditure and your income, the amount left is what you have to spend for that week or month. To try to manage your new income without budgeting will be difficult and probably the route to disaster.

Variable terms and conditions

An important part of your employment package, in addition to your salary or wages, may be the perks (perquisites) provided. Perks will usually be individually negotiated with each employer and his or her employees or their representatives, or just introduced by the employer without consultation or negotiation. They may include such items as a restaurant, perhaps subsidised, luncheon vouchers, company cars, discount for employees buying the company's goods, sports and social clubs, a uniform or a good pension scheme. It is important to consider all these items or the lack of them when assessing your earnings from a particular job.

There are many differences between work and school or work and a home environment. Many offices and factories are now pleasant places in which to work, well decorated with nice carpets, good-quality furniture and a high level of new technology. Some organisations will provide tea breaks while others will provide tea and coffee, although employees may be expected to consume these while they continue work.

If you are working in a clerical or secretarial role, you may be given your own office, although it is more likely that you will be working in a large office with other employees. Many school leavers notice the difference of longer hours at work compared with school; also they are required to stay in one place, normally their own desk, for most of the day. This contrasts with school where each lesson may be in a different classroom with a change of venue every 30 or 40 minutes.

Again, school leavers notice the increased responsibility given to them at work compared with school, but also notice that they are responsible for their own work and have to respond to that responsibility in an adult manner. One new starter straight from school commented he found it strange working with people of many different ages and backgrounds. He felt he had to get on with people with whom he had nothing in common other than that they worked for the same organisation. In addition, at school most pupils wear some kind of uniform, whereas at work there is more freedom of choice, although one is still expected to look the part. Of course, there are many jobs where, for reasons of safety, smartness, keeping clean or public presentation, a uniform (or protective clothing) is worn as a condition of employment. The firm will usually provide such clothing free.

Other terms and conditions of employment you will have to check relate to attitudes to trade union membership, time for hospital and doctor's appointments, arrangements laid down in applying for and obtaining promotion, possible availability of additional training and whether the firm encourages you to undertake further education in your own time or on day-release. In some jobs you may have to buy tools or contribute towards a uniform for work. This type of arrangement will be the subject of some kind of rules or procedure within the firm.

Safety and environment

It is worth remembering that a great deal of legislation exists to ensure that your life at work is as safe as possible. The main Acts are:

- Health and Safety at Work Act
- Railway, Shops and Offices Act
- Factories Acts.

These cover various aspects, such as heating, lighting, ventilation and safe working conditions. They are important aspects of work but are not absolute; for instance, some workplaces are not covered by temperature regulations. Of course, safe and enjoyable working conditions are partly up to you and your colleagues.

In addition, the Control of Substances Hazardous to Health Regulations require employers to control the exposure of employees to toxic and other harmful substances while they are at work.

Checklist

- Your job imposes a legal duty to give diligent and reasonable service
- Your contract will be summarised in writing and given to you
- Your contract will also include implied terms
- You may be paid weekly or monthly in arrears, often into your bank account
- Flexible working hours are increasingly available for staff
- You may be able to join a trade union if you wish
- Legislation exists to ensure a safe working environment and to provide compensation if you are unfairly dismissed
- Income tax and other deductions will be taken off your gross pay to produce your net or take-home pay.

Chapter 8

Success at Interviews: The Quick-Check Chapter

Even if you have read all this book (and especially if you have not), we thought you would appreciate a revision chapter. You can easily read through it before the interview and revise how you should tackle the task ahead.

Background preparation

Keep the following close by you to take to the interview:

- A copy of your application form (you will look silly if you forget what you wrote and you are asked a question about it)
- A copy of your letter of application if there was one
- The letter inviting you to the interview (it helps to be able to show this at the reception office/gatehouse)
- A map of the location if you have been given one
- The company summary that you have compiled or been given
- Any job description you have of the job you are after.

Dry run visit

A dry run trip is an excellent idea if the location is strange to you. Do not be afraid of going right to the door of the establishment. If someone asks what you want, just say something like, 'I am coming for an interview tomorrow and I just wanted to make sure I knew the place.'

This pre-visit avoids panic when you cannot find the way and also stops you being late. On the day you will arrive more relaxed than you would otherwise.

Practice interview

It is extremely helpful if you can practise out loud what you are going to say. A friend or teacher if you are at school can also help by having a mock (ie practice) interview. This will get your mind ready for the type of questions you might well be asked.

Personal preparation

Make sure you are neat, tidy and clean and that your appearance is acceptable (no jeans for an office/shop job). Hair and fingernails should be clean. Modern hair styles are allowed, but there are limits.

This may sound trivial but they are all signs to a prospective employer that you care enough about getting the job to take the trouble to be tidy.

The interview

Remember the key points:

Do not

- Interrupt or argue
- Be negative
- Stare at the floor or out of the window
- Criticise your present boss/teacher
- Smoke or accept a cup of tea/coffee.

Do

- Look at the interviewer(s) – but don't stare
- Answer questions asked
- Develop your answer – avoid 'Yes' and 'No' answers
- Show your preparation (eg company notes and job-hunting log)
- Concentrate on what you can do.

Questions to expect

You must have thought through a number of key questions and have well-practised answers that flow off your tongue. Questions will come in various guises but include:

- Why do you want this job?
- What can you contribute?

- Where do you see yourself going?

You should expect questions about your strengths (and develop these) but also anticipate how you will answer questions that probe any weaknesses (eg lack of experience or exams failure). A good positive reply will work wonders. If you cannot think of a reply, ask friends for advice.

Questions to ask

Make a note on a postcard of any points you feel should be covered before the interview and take the card with you - if you forget, look at it when you need to. Salary, conditions, hours and days of work and training are examples of what you need to know. You should also be ready for the interviewer's 'Have you any questions you wish to ask us?' at the end.

Do not say 'No'!

At the least you should say something like, 'I had a number of points in mind but we have covered them; so all I wish to say is that I would be pleased to get the job and look forward to hearing from you.'

It can help, however, to ask one or two short questions without overstaying your welcome.

What will the interview be like?

Remember, 15–45 minutes is normal for an interview so do not expect a long session.

Many people are surprised by the experience of an interview. There may be exceptions, but by and large you can expect a small number of interviewers (say, one or two in a smaller company and one or two managers plus a personnel officer in a larger company).

The atmosphere will be friendly, helpful and informal. These days the severe, gauntlet-running session is not used. In our experience, only school and more senior local authority appointments adopt this approach, usually supported by large numbers in attendance. This often arises because of the need to have all elected groups present; in school this could mean, in addition to the head, county, parish or borough representatives, governors, parent governors all being present. A frightening (and inefficient) prospect.

Waiting your turn

This may be a tense moment, especially if you have arrived too early. All you can do is try to relax. It is not a good idea to run lots of ideas and questions through your head just before going into the room – you will risk becoming confused which will increase the likelihood of your mind going blank.

Remember: the easiest way to relax and compose yourself is to sit with your feet on the floor side by side:

- Do not cross your legs
- Put your hands on your lap/knees with fingers lightly touching (do not clench)
- Breathe slowly and deeply
- Gaze observantly without staring.

What they are looking for

The interviewer(s) will probably be making notes and may use a form, but either way will be comparing you with their ideal candidate on the following list:

- Appearance/speech
- Enthusiasm/motivation/drive/ambition
- Education, training, qualifications
- Experience and knowledge of the job
- Promotability
- Intellect/imagination
- Personality – will we like him/her?

Try to make sure you bring out your strengths in those areas.

Finally . . .

Do not worry; interviewers know that you are nervous and any nervy slips will not count against you.

And if you fail exams and are having difficulty getting a job? If you are young, consider YT seriously. Qualifications can help but they are not everything so do not be depressed if you don't achieve the best grades in those GCSEs! Employers are as interested in character . . . .

So give of your best and good luck!

Appendix

1. Useful Contacts

- School Careers Adviser
- County Careers Adviser
- Careers Service
- Careers conventions
- Local Jobcentres
- Department of Social Security
- Department of Employment
- Department of Trade and Industry
- Chamber of Commerce
- *Directory of Opportunities for School Leavers* (from local library)
- Advisory, Conciliation and Arbitration Service (ACAS).

2. Further Reading from Kogan Page

The A-Z of Careers and Jobs, 6th edition, ed Diane Burston, 1994

Great Answers to Tough Interview Questions, 3rd edition, Martin John Yate, 1992

How to Pass A Levels and GNVQs, 3rd edition, Howard Barlow, 1995

How to Pass Selection Tests, Mike Bryon and Sanjay Modha, 1991

How to Pass Technical Selection Tests, Mike Bryon and Sanjay Modha, 1993

How to Study, Anne Howe, 1986

How You Can Get That Job! Rebecca Corfield, 1992

The Job Assault Course: A Guide to Civilian Employment for Service Personnel, M C Lindsay Stewart, 1992

The Job Hunter's Handbook, David Greenwood, 1995

Preparing Your Own CV, Rebecca Corfield, 1990

Successful Interview Skills, Rebecca Corfield, 1992

Index